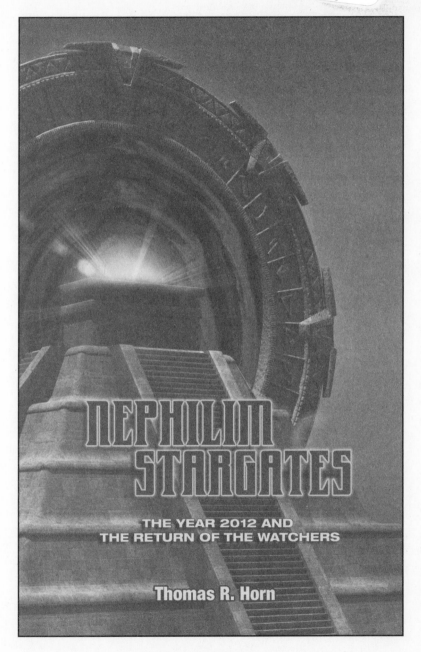

NEPHILIM STARGATES

THE YEAR 2012 AND THE RETURN OF THE WATCHERS

Thomas R. Horn

ANOMALOS PUBLISHING
Crane

NEPHILIM STARGATES
The Year 2012 and the Return of the Watchers

Anomalos Publishing House, Crane 65633
©2007 by Anomalos Publishing House
All rights reserved. Published 2007
Printed in the United States of America.
08   3

ISBN: 0978845315 (paper)
EAN: 9780978845315 (paper)

Author Contact:
www.RaidersNewsNetwork.com

Chapter 6 contains a slightly revised version of "An Occult Translation of the Roswell Event: Count Down to 2012," reprinted with the permission of David E. Flynn and Raiders News Network.

Library of Congress Cataloging-in-Publication Data

Horn, Thomas Nephilim Stargates: The Year 2012 and the Return of the Watchers
   p.cm.

Cover illustration and design by Steve Warner

*More and more we are finding that mythology in general...
very often has some historic base. And the interesting thing
is that one myth which occurs over and over again in
many parts of the world is that somewhere a long time ago
supernatural beings had sexual intercourse with natural
women and produced a special breed of people.*

—FRANCIS A. SCHAEFFER

Contents

Introduction

Something alarming has been happening since the dawn of time, which has been recorded in the history, holy books, and mythos of every great civilization. Ancient rabbinical authorities including Septuagint translators and early church fathers understood it. Sumerians, Assyrians, Egyptians, Greeks, the Hindus, the American Indians, and virtually all other civilizations throughout history believed it. Beings of super intelligence sometimes referred to as "gods" have since time immemorial descended through openings of sky, earth, and sea to interact with this planet's creatures. The behavior of these "unknowns" is recurrent and seems to revolve around the need to harvest or manipulate molecular matter, especially human and animal. The unknowns appear to come to us from nearby planets and/or dimensions and may actually be represented by the Watchers of Apocryphal texts. As mankind expands beyond earth, eons-old ruins of artificial structures or active sites belonging to these ultraterrestrials could be discovered. Such is rumored to exist on Mars and on the dark side of the moon. During the Apollo missions, Neil Armstrong reportedly mentioned seeing "strange lights" on the moon and said, "We have company," before Mission Control switched off the live feed. Former NASA employee Otto Binder gave sworn testimony concerning that transmission and said it was picked up by numerous ham radio operators as Apollo 11 entered the Sea of Tranquility:

> *Mission Control:* What's there?…Mission control
> calling APOLLO 11.

> *Apollo 11:* These babies are huge, sir…enormous….
> You wouldn't believe it! I'm telling you there are
> other spacecraft out there…lined up on the far side
> of the crater edge…they're on the moon watching
> us….(Good 384)

Otto's testimony was supported by others in government including the former chief of NASA communication systems, Maurice Chatelain, who claimed *the encounter "was common knowledge in NASA, but nobody has talked about it until now."* Christopher Kraft, the former director of NASA's Houston tracking base at the time, is credited with releasing related Mission Control transcript information following his retirement:

> *Apollo 11:* Those are giant things. No, no, no…this is
> not an optical illusion. No one is going to believe
> this!

> *Mission Control (Center):* What…what…what? What
> is happening? What's wrong with you?

> *Apollo 11:* They're here under the surface.

> *Mission Control:* What's there? Emission inter-
> rupted…interference control calling Apollo 11.

> *Apollo 11:* We saw some visitors. They were there for
> awhile, observing the instruments.

> *Mission Control:* Repeat your last information.

Apollo 11: I say that there were other spaceships. They're lined up on the other side of the crater.

Mission Control: Repeat...repeat!

Apollo 11: Let us sound this orbit a...In 625 to... automatic relay connected...My hands are shaking so badly I can't do anything. Film it?

Mission Control: Have you picked up anything?

Apollo 11: I didn't have any film at hand. Three shots of the saucers or whatever they were that were ruining the film.

Mission Control: Control, control here. Are you on your way? Is the uproar with the UFO's? Over?

Apollo 11: They've landed there. There they are, and they are watching us.

Mission Control: The mirrors, the mirrors...have you set them up?

Apollo 11: Yes, they're in the right place. But whoever made those space ships surely can come tomorrow and remove them.

Did Apollo astronauts actually catch a glimpse of the Watchers? Did Armstrong really say, "They're on the moon watching us"? Has testimony from equally reputable members of the government, military, and scientific community, including five former US presidents, verified as substantial fact that something has been seen, felt, and recorded throughout history (beginning with the first known written records) watching us, interacting with us, and coming through portals to pursue causes we may not yet understand? *Nephilim Stargates: The Year 2012 and the Return of the Watchers* is a glimpse into this past, present, and future phenomena, with an eye on what sages and scientists believe and what futurists and prophets may yet fear.

Chapter 1

PIECES OF TRUTH: MYTHOLOGY

Most people at some time during their life discover striking similarities between Christianity and the world's most ancient religions. Some use this to discredit the Hebrew faith, claiming that stories from the Old Testament, especially the record of Creation and the epic of Noah's Flood, were borrowed from earlier Sumerian cosmology. In response, I postulated a theory called "Original Revelation" in my second book *The Gods Who Walk Among Us* to explain the parallelism within Sumerian, Hebrew, Greek, and Egyptian religion. I theorized that a perfect revelation was given from the Creator to man "in the beginning." The first man was at one with God and perceived divine knowledge from the mind of God. The human was "in tune" with the mental processes of God and understood, therefore, what God knew about science, astronomy, cosmogony, geology, eschatology, etc.

In Hebrew and Christian tradition, after Adam fell, he was "detached" from the mind of God but retained an imperfect memory of the divine revelation, including a knowledge of God's plan of redemption. Two things began to occur in the decades following this separation. Information from the original revelation became distant and distorted as it was dispersed among nations and passed from generation to generation by oral tradition, and second, evil supernaturalism seized upon the opportunity to receive worship and to turn people away from Yahweh by distorting and counterfeiting the original revelation with pagan ideas and "gods." This point of view is the choice of some scholars when considering that the earliest history and archeological records from civilizations around the world attest to what appears to be a singular and original story.

In their startling book *The Discovery of Genesis: How the Truths of Genesis Were Found Hidden in the Chinese Language,* the Rev. C.H. Kang and Dr. Ethel R. Nelson confirm that prehistoric Chinese ideographic pictures (used in very ancient Chinese writing) report the story of Genesis, including the creation of the man and woman, the garden, the temptation and Fall, Noah's Flood, and the Tower of Babel.

In his book *The Real Meaning Of The Zodiac,* Dr. James Kennedy claims that the ancient signs of the Zodiac indicate a singular and original revelation—a kind of Gospel in the stars—and that the message of the stars, although converted into astrology later, originally recorded the Gospel. According to Kennedy:

> There exists in the writings of virtually all civilized nations a description of the major stars in the heavens— something which might be called their "Constellations of the Zodiac" or the "Signs of the Zodiac," of which there are twelve. If you go back in time to Rome, or beyond that to Greece, or before that to Egypt, Persia, Assyria,

or Babylonia—regardless of how far back you go, there is a remarkable phenomenon: Nearly all nations had the same twelve signs, representing the same twelve things, placed in the same order....The book of Job, which is thought by many to be the oldest book of the Bible, goes back to approximately 2150 BC, which is 650 years before Moses came upon the scene to write the Pentateuch; over 1,100 years before Homer wrote the *Odyssey* and the *Illiad*; and 1,500 years before Thales, the first of the philosophers, was born. In Chapter 38, God finally breaks in and speaks to Job and to his false comforters. As He is questioning Job, showing him and his companions their ignorance, God says to them: "Canst thou bind the sweet influences of Pleiades, or loose the bands of Orion? Canst thou bring forth Mazzaroth in his season? Or canst thou guide Arcturus with his sons?" (Job 38.31-32). We see here reference to the constellations of Orion and Pleiades, and the star Arcturus. Also in the book of Job there is reference to *Cetus*, the *Sea Monster*, and to *Draco, the Great Dragon*. I would call your attention to Job 38.32a: "Canst thou bring forth Mazzaroth in his season?" *Mazzaroth* is a Hebrew word which means "The Constellations of the Zodiac." In what may be the oldest book in all of human history, we find that the constellations of the zodiac were already clearly known and understood.... Having made it clear that the Bible expressly, explicitly, and repeatedly condemns what is now known as astrology, the fact remains that there was a God-given Gospel [*universally acknowledged original revelation*] in the stars which lays beyond and behind that which has now been corrupted. (Kennedy 6-8)

Thus, Dr. Kennedy asserts that the constellations of the zodiac were likely given by God to the first man as "record-keepers" of the original revelation. If the assumption of this view is correct—that an original revelation degenerated into global mythology following a break in the relationship between Creator and creation—one should be able to find numerous examples of mythological stories from as far back as the beginning of history and within various civilizations around the world that are actually based on an original revelation. Since the myths behind the gods would thus be "borrowed" ideas, the corrupted texts would be similar to the original truth and, in that sense, evidence that a singular and original revelation existed.

WHEN MYTHOLOGY
IS MORE THAN MYTH

In Matthew, Jesus Christ said he would build his church, "... and the gates of hell shall not prevail against it" (King James Version, Mt.16.18). Putting the word "hell" in context here is important because while the later meaning of the Greek word transliterated "Hades" was confused with death and the grave (Thanatos [also see Rev. 1.18]), at the time Jesus chose to use this word, he was referring to the person of Hades or Pluto, the god of the lower regions, and Orcus, the nether world and realm of the dead. This brings up a very important question. Why would Jesus mention a Greek deity, as if Hades were a personal, sentient combatant if there were nothing more to this story than myth? In my opinion it was because He knew the true story behind the mythological gods. He knew their real identity and the measure of their power.

ANCIENT RECORDS
AND WHAT THEY CAN TELL US

In Hesiod's Theogony we learn of the twelve pre-Olympian gods known as the Titans, who ruled the Universe. The Titans were the children of Gaia, who gave birth to these "elder" gods by cohabiting with Uranus. The important Titans included Oceanus, Tethys, Mnemosyne, Themis, Hyperion, Iapetus, and Atlas. When Uranus attempted to imprison the Titans within the body of his wife Gaia (the earth), Cronus, the youngest and most terrible of her children, conspired with his mother and castrated Uranus with a sickle. The mutilation of Uranus separated Heaven from Earth and succeeded in freeing the Titans. When the powerful Cronus later cast the severed genitals of his father into the sea, a white foam enveloped them, and from this foam, Aphrodite was born (thus, the name derived from "aphros," which means "sea foam").

As the newly crowned king of the gods, Cronus married his sister Rhea. Six famous god-children were born of their union: Hestia, Demeter, Hera, (Hades,) Poseidon, and Zeus. Mother Gaia and Father Uranus warned Cronus that his offspring would someday try to overthrow and replace him as the king of the gods. Cronus therefore attempted to circumvent the possibility of threat by swallowing each child whole as it was born. Rhea was displeased and replaced baby Zeus with a cloth-wrapped stone, which Cronus unwittingly swallowed instead. She then hid Zeus at Crete where he was fed on the milk of the goat Amalthaea and remained until adulthood, protected by the nymphs.

Years later, Zeus made Cronus regurgitate his brothers and sisters. A fierce ten-year war ensued, and the younger, more powerful Olympians overthrew the elder Titans and cast them down into Tartarus (a place in the underworld, even lower than Hades) where they (except for Hecate) were to remain fettered forever. Eventually Zeus reconciled with the Titans and proclaimed Cronus the ruler of the Golden Age. Meanwhile he summoned his brothers, Hades and Poseidon, and decreed that the universe should thereafter be divided among them. The sky became the dominion of Zeus; Poseidon was chosen to rule over the sea; and the inner earth, or underworld, was declared the haunt of Hades. The surface of the earth was determined neutral grounds—a place where sky, sea, and underworld joined and where all deities could merge.

The concept that sky, sea, and underworld are inhabited by "gods" who use the earth as a mutual gathering ground, door, or path between dimensional realities is important and is repeated in the mythos and holy books of cultures around the world, including, as we shall see later, the Bible.

HOW THE "MYSTERY" SCHOOLS ILLUSTRATED EARTH AS A SPIRIT AXIS OF SKY, SEA, AND UNDERWORLD

The Thesmophoria was the most popular of the ancient Greek fertility festivals. Held in honor of Demeter—whose cult secrets were the most protected of the mystery religions—the rituals were performed inside of the inner sanctum of the Temple of Demeter (the Telesterion) and were so well-guarded by the Temple devotees that little survived to enlighten us as to what actually occurred there. Only those portions of the Thesmophoria held outside the Temple were recorded, providing a sparse historical record.

What is known is that the rituals of the Thesmophoria were based on the mythology of the abduction and rape of

Persephone (Proserpina) and on the mythology of Demeter's (Persephone's mother) subsequent actions in searching for her daughter. The cult's rituals, therefore, are interpreted according to the Demeter myth, which claimed that Hades—the dark god of the underworld—fell in love with beautiful Persephone.

According to the myth, one day as Persephone plucked flowers in a grassy meadow, Hades swooped down in his chariot and dragged her into the underworld, where he forced her to become his bride. Above ground, Demeter was distraught by her daughter's disappearance and searched the earth in vain to find her. With the help of Helios and Hecate, Demeter finally discovered the truth about what had happened. In her fury, she demanded Hades release her daughter. When he refused, she sent horrific famine upon the earth. Plants dried up, seeds refused to sprout, and the gods began to suffer from a lack of sacrifices.

Finally, Zeus dispatched Hermes to intercede with the lord of the underworld. After great debate, Hades agreed to release Persephone if she would eat a pomegranate seed. What Persephone did not understand was that by eating the pomegranate seed in the mystical location of the underworld, divine symmetry was created that bonded her with Hades. This ensured that the goddess would automatically return to the underworld for a third part of each year (in the winter) during which time the seeds of the ground would not grow. Persephone thus became the Upper World goddess of youth and happiness and the underworld queen of the dead; a dual role that depicted her as both good and evil. On earth she was the goddess of the young and the friend of the nymphs who appeared in the blooming of the spring flowers (symbolizing her annual return from Hades), and in the underworld she was the dreaded wife of Hades and the Queen of Darkness who controlled the fates of deceased men.

The reenactment of such myth—the abduction and rape of Persephone—was central to the rituals of the Thesmophoria and, as such, key to interpreting the bits of information known about the mystical importance of the rituals. The festival of the Thesmophoria—sometimes called the Eleusinian Mysteries—lasted between three and ten days. Each day of the festival had a different name and included specific rites. A highlight of the festival was a procession from Athens to Eleusis, which was led by a crowd of children known as ephebi. The ephebi assisted in carrying the hiera (sacred objects), in pulling a statue of Dionysus as a boy (Iacchus), and finally in facilitating the ceremonial cleansing of the initiates (candidates of the mystery religion) in the sea.

Upon arriving at Eleusis, the women organized the first day of the celebration (anodos) by building temporary shelters and electing the leaders of the camp. On the second day (nesteia) they initiated the Greater Mysteries which, according to myth, produced the cult's magical requests (a fertile harvest). Such mysteries included a parody of the abduction and rape of Persephone and the positioning of the female devotees upon the ground weeping (in the role of Demeter for her daughter) as well as fasting for the return of Persephone (the return of spring). The setting upon the ground and fasting also intended to transfer the "energies" of the women into the ground and thus, into the fall seeds. On the fifth day of the festival, the participants drank a special grain mixture called kykeon (a symbol of Persephone) in an attempt to assimilate the spirit of the goddess. The idea was to produce an incarnated blessing of fertility in both crops and children.

About this same time, certain women called "antleriai" were cleansed in the sea and sent down into the mountainside trenches to recover sacrificial piglets and various other sacred objects that had been thrown into the hillside canyons several days before. The piglets, along with the sacred objects (which included dough replicas of snakes and genitalia), then were burned with a grain-seed mixture as an offering to Demeter.

The reason for casting the piglets and the sacred objects into the mountainside cliffs has been thoroughly debated, and no single interpretation has emerged as the final authority. However, interpretations can be made of the symbology of the sacred objects. While the dough replicas of snakes and genitalia are obviously fertility symbols, the pigs' blood was sacred to the gods, and thus, the piglets are the key to understanding the ritual.

Greeks venerated pigs because of their uncanny ability to find and unearth underground items (roots, etc.). Some scholars conclude from this that the ritual casting of the pigs "into the deep" was a form of imitative magic based on the underworld myth of Persephone and Hades. That is to say, casting the piglets into the deep canyon trenches and fetching them out again represented the descent of Persephone into the underworld and her subsequent return to the surface of the earth.

The piglets in the trenches also may have served the practical purpose of supplying a host (body) for Persephone to occupy until the antleriai women could assist her (by retrieving the piglets) in her annual escape from the underworld. Burning the piglets later that night would, according to the ancient religious idea that fire passes the soul from one location to another, free the spirit of Persephone into the Upper World. (This is similar to the children sacrificed to Baal who "passed through the fire" [2 Kings 23.10] from the physical world into the spiritual).

Yet the New Testament's position seems to be that such pagan rituals were the worship of demons: "...the things which the Gentiles sacrifice," Paul says, "they sacrifice to devils..." (1 Cor. 10.20). One could argue that in Luke 8 a connection exists between the ritual casting of the piglets into the deep canyon trenches (representing a descent into hell) and the biblical story of the Gadarene demoniac:

> And they arrived at the country of the Gadarenes.... And when he [Jesus] went forth to land, there met him out of the city a certain man, which had devils.... When he [the demoniac] saw Jesus, he cried out, and fell down before him, and with a loud voice said, What have I to do with thee, Jesus, thou Son of God most high? I beseech thee, torment me not....And Jesus asked him, saying, What is thy name? And he said, Legion: because many devils were entered into him. And they besought him that he would not command them to go out into the deep. And there was there an herd of swine feeding on the mountain: and they besought him that he would suffer them to enter into them. And he suffered them. Then went the devils out of the man, and entered into the swine: and the herd ran violently down a steep place into the sea, and were choked. (Luke 8.26-33)

The word "deep" in this text is Abussos (the Abyss) and refers to the underworld's Bottomless Pit. Since the principle elements of the sea, the swine, and the deep are employed, and since the Abyss (part of the underworld) is central to the narrative; and further since the cult rituals of the Thesmophoria were well known throughout Asia Minor and were considered by the Hebrews to be the activity of the devil (the inhabitants of Hades were known as "Demeter's people," and Hecate, the goddess of witchcraft, was Persephone's underworld guide during the rituals); one could easily surmise that Jesus is either mocking the Thesmophoria or revealing to His followers that such rituals were the consort of devils. It may be a stretch to interpret the biblical story in this way, but clearly the similarities and historical proximities are startling, especially given that the demons requested entry into the swine.

Why would demons make such a plea? There are two possible connections with the Thesmophoria: 1) the demons believe that by entering the swine they could escape the underworld deep (as in the magical Persephone escape ritual described above), and 2) Jesus, by granting the request of the devils, is illustrating that the Thesmophoria ritual of casting piglets into the deep is inherently demonic. Obviously there are other possible interpretations of the narrative. Yet, since this is the only record of Jesus granting the petition of demons, it seems possible that a powerful social commentary on a popular pagan idea, such as the Thesmophoria of Demeter, is made by Christ.

ONCE UPON A TIME, THERE WAS THIS TITAN THAT ESCAPED HELL

Hecate, the Titan earth-mother of the wizards and witches, illustrates, perhaps better than Demeter, the connection between the sky, the earth, the underworld, and the realm of evil supernaturalism. As the daughter of Perses and Asteria, Hecate was the only Titan to remain free under Zeus. She was characterized by the unknown and by the night-terrors that roamed the abandoned and desolate highways.

Other interesting facts about Hecate include:

- Hecate was often depicted as a young maiden with three faces, each pointing in a different direction—a role in which she was the earth-spirit that haunted wherever three paths joined. As the "goddess of three forms," she was Luna (the moon) in heaven, Diana (Artemis) on earth, and Hecate of the underworld.

- At midnight, Hecate's devotees would leave food offerings at intersections for the goddess (Hecate's Supper) and, once deposited, quickly exit without turning around or looking back. Sometimes the offerings consisted of honey cakes and chicken hearts, while at other times, puppies and female black lambs were slaughtered and mixed with honey for the goddess and her strigae. (Strigae) were deformed owl-like affiliates of Hecate who flew through the night feeding on the bodies of unattended babies. During the day, they appeared as simple old women—folklore that may account for the history of flying witches. The strigae hid amidst the leaves of the trees during the annual festival of Hecate, held on August 13, when Hecate's followers offered up the highest praise of the goddess).

- Hecate's devotees celebrated with festivals near Lake Averna in Campania, where the sacred willow groves of the goddess stood, and they communed with the tree spirits (earth spirits, including Hecate, were thought to inhabit trees) and summoned the souls of the dead from the mouths of nearby caves. It was here that Hecate was known as Hecate-Chthonia, (Hecate of the earth), a depiction in which she most clearly embodied the popular earth-mother-spirit that communicated by channeling through the cave stones and sacred willow trees. *new age*

Yet Hecate had other, more revealing titles, and these names are the subject of interest for the time being: 1) Hecate-

Phosphoros ("The Light Bearer"); and 2) Hecate-Propylaia ("The One Who Guards the Gate").

The idea that mythological deities were perceived as guarding gates (and in some cases imprisoned behind them) and that often these gods and goddesses were known by ancients as "light bearers" is interesting in view of Scripture. The Hebrew translation of the word "Lucifer" means "light bearer," and the New Testament speaks of Satan being "transformed into an angel of light" (2 Cor. 11.14). A deeper study of scripture supports the idea that spiritual forces that exist behind barriers or "gates" are located in the sky, sea, and physical earth. For instance, the book of Ephesus is a study of principalities and powers in "high places" and "powers of the air." In Nehemiah 9.6 the prophet speaks of more than one heaven: he saw the heavens and the "heaven of heavens." These are peripheral heavens or divisions as Paul refers to in 2 Cor. 12.2, saying, "I knew a man in Christ above fourteen years ago…[who was] caught up to the third heaven." As a Pharisee, Paul acknowledged three main "heavens," which include a domain of air (the kosmos), or height, controlled by Satan (Ahriman in Zoroastrianism). In pharisaical thought, the first heaven is simply the place where the birds fly, anything removed from and not attached to the surface of the earth. On the other end of the spectrum and of a different substance is the third heaven—the dwelling place of God. This is the place from which angelic spheres spread outward. Between the first heaven where the birds fly and the third heaven where the Throne of God was believed to be, was a war zone called the second heaven. This is a place of brass gates (see The Apocalypse of Zephaniah)—the kosmos or Hebrew equivalent of the Persian *Ahriman-abad* —the place where Satan or Beelzebul (the "lord of the height") abides as the prince of the power of the "air" (aer, the lower air, circumambient). This war zone is a sort of gasket heaven, the domain of Satan encompassing the surface of the earth. It was believed that from here powerful demons known as kosmokrators could overshadow cities, intrude upon, and attempt to influence the affairs and governments of men. It was also believed that from the kosmos Satan's minions also sought to close the gateways above cities so that God's blessings could not flow into them. Later, it was believed that when saints bent their knees in prayer, they had to pray through walls/gates of opposition contained within this gasket heaven.

In addition to heavenly gateways behind which fallen spirits dwell, Jon. 2.6 tells of Jonah going down to the bottom of the sea into a "city of gates" (Hebrew B@riyach, a fortress in the earth, a prison) from which God delivered him. There is no doubt about where Jonah was as he prayed to God in Jon. 2.2 "out of the belly of hell" (Sheol—the underworld prison of the dead). This text is both fascinating and illuminating when compared to the words of Christ in Matt. 16.17-18: "Blessed art thou, Simon Barjona [son of Jonah]…thou art Peter, and upon this rock I will build my church; and the gates of hell shall not prevail against it." Matthew's unique choice of words connecting the rock upon which the church would be built, the name of Jonah, and the gates of hell is not a coincidence. Christ made the same connection to hell's gateway, Jonah, and his mission for the Church in Matt. 12.40: "For as Jonas was three days and three nights in the whale's belly; so shall the Son of man be three days and three nights in the heart of the earth."

In addition to Jonah and Christ, the Bible refers to non-human entities in subterraneous locations as well. For instance, "the four angels which are bound in the great river Euphrates" (Rev. 9.14). Job 26.5 tells of the Rafa (Rephaim, fallen angels or offspring of such) who writhe "beneath the waters" (Interlinear Hebrew and Youngs Literal Translation). 2 Pet. 2.4 and Jude 6 indicate that the subsurface earth is a prison or holding tank where God has bound certain fallen entities, etc.

Furthermore, Deut. 18.11 warns that such spirits might seek to move beyond their confines through human intervention or invitation. The Hebrew people were warned not to communicate with these spirits, and when the witch of Endor did so, they ascended up from "out of the earth" (1 Sam. 28.13).

Based on such texts, it is reasonable to believe that beings of superintelligence sometimes referred to as "gods" are equivalent to those whom the Bible depicts as moving through openings of sky, earth, and sea during interaction with this planet's creatures. Some of these multidimensionals are more restrained than others, yet in most cases they can by invitation "ascend" or transcend these gateways, presenting themselves as "light bearers" or "angels of light."

Chapter 2

THROUGH THE GATES

The story in 1 Sam. 28 makes reference to the beings that ascended up from "out of the earth" as "gods" (1 Sam. 28.13). When Saul asked the woman with the "familiar spirit" (1 Sam. 28.7) what had scared her so much, she answered, "I saw gods ascending out of the earth" (1 Sam. 28.13). The Endorian witch may have identified one of these "gods" as the deceased Samuel, but many Christians are uncomfortable with the idea of communicating with the dead and insist the reference had to be to something else. Exactly what else this being might have been is the question.

THE AMALANTRAH WORKING

In 1918, famed occultist Aleister Crowley attempted to create a dimensional vortex that would bridge the gap between the world of the seen and the unseen. The ritual was called the Amalantrah Working and according to Crowley became successful when a presence manifested itself through the rift. He called the being "Lam" and drew a portrait of it. The startling

21

image, detailed almost ninety years ago, bears powerful similarity with "Alien Greys" of later pop culture.

Nearly three decades after the Amalantrah Working, rocket scientist and cofounder of the Jet Propulsion Laboratory Jack Parsons and his pal L. Ron Hubbard (Church of Scientology founder) conducted a second ritual, the "Babalon Working," in an attempt to reopen the gateway created by Crowley. The two men were not seeking audience with Lam. Instead they wanted the spirit of Babylon, the archetypal divine feminine, to pass through the portal and to incarnate itself within a human being. Many adepts of Enochian magic and Ordo Templi Orientis believe they succeeded and that she—the whore of Babylon—walks the earth today. It would come as no surprise, as Babylonian and earlier "gods" have been depicted as coming through "gates" for some time.

DEFINING THE GODS OF GATEWAYS

A popular hypothesis, sometimes called the Ancient Astronaut theory, claims that superintelligent beings have been visiting the earth through dimensional gates for eons. According to the theory, these are "the gods of mythology" and are responsible for creating the human species. In the introduction to his bestselling book, *Chariots of the Gods?*, Erich von Däniken, who, it might be argued, is a father of the ancient astronaut theory, says:

> I claim that our forefathers received visits from the universe in the remote past, even though I do not yet know who these extraterrestrial intelligences were or from which planet they came. I nevertheless proclaim that these "strangers" annihilated part of mankind existing at the time and produced a new, perhaps the first, Homo sapiens. (10)

As was illustrated in the Hollywood films, *Contact* and *Close Encounters of the Third Kind,* von Däniken's premise took America by storm in the 1960s with the proposition that mankind was possibly the offspring of an ancient, perhaps ongoing, extraterrestrial experiment. Ufologists like Däniken assert that the gods of the mythological record may have been evidence of, and a reaction to, encounters with other-world beings. According to such theorists, ancient men would have considered space travelers as gods and would have recorded, via hieroglyphs, megaliths, and stone tablets, these space travelers' arrival, experiments, and departure as a "supernatural" encounter between gods and men. Mr. Däniken continues:

> While [the] spaceship disappears again into the mists of the universe our friends will talk about the miracle— "The gods were here!"…they will make a record of what happened: uncanny, weird, miraculous. Then their texts will relate—and drawings will show—that gods in golden clothes were there in a flying boat that landed with a tremendous din. They will write about chariots which the gods drove over land and sea, and of terrifying weapons that were like lightning, and they will recount that the gods promised to return. They will hammer and chisel in the rock pictures of what they had seen: shapeless giants with helmets and rods on their heads, carrying boxes in front of their chests; balls on which indefinable beings sit and ride through the air; staves from which rays are shot out as if from a sun…(26)

Von Däniken also says the odd appearance of some of the gods as depicted in various hieroglyphs (human-like creatures with falcon heads, lions with heads of bulls, etc.) could be viewed as evidence of "aliens" genetically modifying ancient people and animals to create transgenic life-forms. Some accept this as an alternative to the biblical account of creation and believe similar activity continues via "abduction" by small, typically Grey "aliens," who supposedly pilot UFOs and conduct various experiments on unwilling victims. Such activity is seen as the malevolent relationship between certain humans and these "gods" of creation. Radical aspects of their procedures often include impregnating abductees and later removing hybrid embryos. It is uncertain how many support this theory, but approximately eighty percent of Americans alone believe in the possibility of extraterrestrial life. Some, like the thirty-nine members of the Heaven's Gate cult, who committed suicide in Rancho Santa Fe, California, and who believed they were being summoned by a UFO trailing the Hale-Bopp Comet, subscribe to an eerie amalgam of mysticism and conventional religion.

no Kidding...

DÄNIKEN IS RIGHT:
THERE HAVE BEEN STRANGE VISITORS

According to the Bible:

> When mankind had spread all over the world, and girls were being born, some of the supernatural beings saw that these girls were beautiful, so they took the ones they liked....In those days, and even later, there were giants [Nephilim] on the earth who were descendants of human women and the supernatural beings. (Today's English Version, Gen. 6.4)

Regardless of one's interpretation of this particular verse, thousands of years ago heavenly beings visited the earth. They engaged in experiments resulting in a race of mutant offspring called Nephilim. In the New Testament, Jesus Christ speaks of these days (of Noah) as being comparable to the time leading up to his return and to the end of the age (Matt. 24.37). Are current "UFO" visitors, and resultant abductions and experiments, the same as those of Noah's day? If so, why have heavenly beings visited (and continue visiting) the earth, and what is this genetic tinkering with creation about?

One theory says when the protoevangelium was given (the promise that the seed of the woman would produce a child who would crush the serpent's head), supernatural beings, perhaps aliens or fallen angels, appeared from heaven and performed genetic alterations on human DNA to intercept, pollute, and cut off the birth line of the Messiah. As Pharaoh destroyed the Hebrew children so that the deliverer might not be born, as Herod sought baby Jesus in order to have him killed, as the dragon of Revelation 12 waits to destroy the seed of the woman as soon as it is born, so too some believe Satan wanted to stop the promised seed by sending supernatural beings to alter the human race.

Yet my friend I.D.E. Thomas in his book *The Omega Conspiracy: Satan's Last Assault on God's Kingdom* says Satan had additional plans to kill off the Messiah. According to Thomas, Satan (as opposed to aliens) was trying to produce a race of mutant warriors to exterminate the Jewish race and, worse, to genetically alter creation from the image of God to one of Satan's own.

From Thomas's point of view, this explains why people like the Sumerians of Mesopotamia, whose legends preceded much Hebrew folklore, brought with them a pantheon of deities, and why subsequent religions adopted similar ideas of powerful beings—with names like "Zeus" and "Apollo"—who visited the earth, marrying women, and fathering half-human children.

"THEY" (THOSE WHO HAVE COME THROUGH THE "GATES") WERE ALSO CALLED "WATCHERS"

The Ancient Astronaut theory and the teaching of theologians alike look to the prehistoric legend of Watchers (mysterious beings who first appeared in the early cultures of the Middle East) to discuss the Anunnaki (Sumerian Gods), Nephilim (giants referenced in Gen. 6.4), and the creation of mutant DNA following earth visitations by "gods." We find:

- The Egyptians originally migrated from the biblical land of Shinar, which means "the Land of the Watchers." The Egyptians called it *Ta Neter*—"The Land of the Watchers"—"from which the gods came into Egypt."
- In the *Book of the Dead* (Plates 7-10) there are prayers for deliverance from the Watchers (Tchatcha, the princes of Osiris), who came from Ta-Ur (the Far Away Land).
- The Sumerian scribes referred to the Watchers as Anunnaki, which, they said, "came from Nibiru" to judge/rule the inhabitants of the earth. Some interpret this Nibiru as "a distant planet" while others say it should be translated, "Those Who from Heaven to Earth Came."
- The Bible refers to Nephilim, which also means those who came from Heaven to Earth.
- In the Book of Jubilees—a.k.a. the Apocalypse of Moses—the Watchers are compared to supernatural beings mentioned in the sixth chapter of Genesis.

- The Apocryphal Book of Enoch associates the creatures of Genesis 6 with the Watchers:

> And I Enoch was blessing the Lord of majesty and the King of the ages, and lo! the Watchers called me—Enoch the scribe—and said to me: "Enoch, thou scribe of righteousness, go, declare to the Watchers of the heaven who have left the high heaven, the holy eternal place, and have defiled themselves with women, and have done as the children of earth do, and have taken unto themselves wives: 'Ye have wrought great destruction on the earth: And ye shall have no peace nor forgiveness of sin: and inasmuch as they delight themselves in their children, The murder of their beloved ones shall they see, and over the destruction of their children shall they lament, and shall make supplication unto eternity, but mercy and peace shall ye not attain.'" (1 Enoch 12.3-6)

- According to the Dead Sea Scrolls, only two hundred of this larger group of powerful beings called "Watchers" departed from the higher Heavens and sinned. Thus, Enoch refers to the Watchers in the High Heavens as separate from the ones on earth. The fallen class of Watchers are considered by some to be the same creatures who in the Book of Jude are called the "angels which kept not their first estate, but left their own habitation...[and are] reserved in everlasting chains under darkness unto the judgment of the great day" (King James Version, Jude 1.6).

After studying this and other ancient records, I.D.E. Thomas concludes that recent "UFO" abduction activity may indicate a return of the servants of the Watchers, the lesser "angels" that followed the two hundred, as we approach the end of the age and the coming of Armageddon. Do biblical and extra-biblical records support the ancient astronaut theory that alien creatures traveled from distant planets or different dimensions and genetically tinkered with Homo sapiens? Were these flying geniuses afterward honored in the images and folklore of the gods of mythology? Or is Thomas correct in that Genesis and similar books are a record of fallen angels acting in accord with Satan?

We may find out sooner than we think. Unexplained phenomena are occurring all around us, and reports of "beings" moving through portals (i.e. ufonauts) are coming in with regular frequency. Whoever or whatever these beings are, the reality of their activity can no longer be doubted.

Chapter 3

ANCIENT GODS: HEROES? WATCHERS? MAGICIANS?

In order to catalogue the beings who have come through the stargates in the past, in the present, and those powerful ones who are perched to do so in the very near future, two primary assumptions are required. (It should be noted that versions of these assumptions are accepted by general camps of Ufology—both those restrictively from the biblical worldview and those outside that view.) These assumptions are:

1. That beings of myth were at least at times based on authentic interaction with superintelligences of unknown origin.
2. That certain mythology as well as anomalous "historical records" were the efforts of men to interpret these eye-witness accounts and visitations.

We begin with the religion of Sumeria, as it was the first known organized mythology and greatly influenced the foundational beliefs of the forthcoming nations of Assyria, Egypt, Greece, Rome, and others. The question of origin of Sumerian belief has interested scholars and historians for more than a millennium. Specifically, where does one find the beginning of the gods of Sumeria? Were the Sumerian deities the product of human imagination, or the distortion of an earlier prehistoric revelation? Were they "mythologized" heroes, or (as subscribers to the Ancient Astronaut theory believe) alien visitors whose appearance gave birth to legends and gods of mythology? More importantly, did the gods of Sumeria reflect the emergence of a real, perhaps spiritual, influence operating through pagan dynamics?

These questions are both fascinating and difficult since the deities of ancient Sumeria/Mesopotamia continue to be shrouded in a history of unknown origins. It was as though from "out of nowhere" the Sumerians sprang onto the scene over 5,500 years ago, bringing with them the first written language and a corpus of progressive knowledge—from complicated religious concepts, to an advanced understanding of astrology, chemistry, and mathematics.

The three common theories regarding the origin of Sumerian myth are: 1) the Euhemerus view, 2) the ancient astronaut view, and 3) the biblical view.

The Euhemerus view is based on the theories of the Greek scholar Euhemerus, who claimed the pagan gods originated with famous ancient kings who were later deified. The more popular theories—the Ancient Astronaut and the biblical view—apply an "event" that is believed to have occurred, during which early humans were visited—perhaps even altered–by superintelligent beings. To some these visitors were "angels" and/or "demons," while to others they were advanced humanoids.

THE BEGINNING

The earliest legends of Sumerian myth begin with the belief in "god" (Anu) as the creator of all things and "ruler of heaven." A later struggle between the "ruler of the heavens" versus the "power of the air" occurred after Enki, the god of wisdom and water, created the human race out of clay. It appears that Anu, who was at first the most powerful of the Sumerian gods and the "ruler of the heavens," was superseded in power and popularity by Enlil, the "god of the air." (To the Christian mind this could be perceived as a record of Satan, the god of the air, continuing his pretence to the throne of God, and his usurpation of Yahweh—"the Lord of the heavens.")

Correspondingly, in the *Enûma Elish* (a Babylonian epic), Marduk, the great god of the city of Babylon, was exalted above the benevolent gods and extolled as the creator of the world. Marduk was symbolized as a dragon called the Muscrussu, and his legend also appears to contain several similarities of the biblical account of creation. The *Adapa Epic* likewise tells a Babylonian legend roughly equivalent to the Genesis account of creation. In it, Adapa, like Adam, underwent a test on food consumption, failed the test and forfeited his opportunity for immortality. As a result of the failure, suffering and death were passed along to humanity.

Finally, in the *Epic of Gilgamesh* one can find startling similarities to the biblical Flood record deeply rooted in ancient Assyrian and Babylonian mythology. In 1872, George Smith discovered the Gilgamesh tablets while doing research on the Assyrian library of Ashurbanipal at the British Museum. As he interpreted the text, a legend emerged: Gilgamesh, the king of the city of Uruk, was told about a great flood from his immortal friend, Utnapishtim (the Sumerian equivalent of Noah). Utnapishtim described for

Gilgamesh how the great god Enlil had decided to destroy all of mankind because of its sins. Enlil sent a plague which failed to persuade mankind of better behavior. Consequently, the gods determined to exterminate the human race. Enki, the lord of the waters, was not happy with the other gods for this decision and warned Utnapishtim of the coming deluge, instructing him to tear down his house and to build a great boat. Utnapishtim obeyed Enki, built the vessel, and sealed it with pitch and bitumen. The family of Utnapishtim loaded onto the boat together with various beasts and fowl. When the rains came, the doors were closed, and the vessel rose up above the waters. Like Noah, Utnapishtim sent out a dove, and later a swallow, to search for dry land. They both returned. Later, a raven was released, and it never came back. After several more days the boat came to rest on the top of a mountain where Utnapishtim built an altar and offered a sacrifice of thanksgiving to the gods. As the gods smelt the sweet offering, all but Enlil repented for sending the flood. For over a hundred years the story of Gilgamesh was considered by many to be nothing more than myth. Then, in April of 2003, archaeologists in Iraq announced the discovery of what they believed to be the lost tomb of King Gilgamesh—the subject of the oldest "book" in history.

Scholars began to wonder: if Gilgamesh actually lived, should anything be made of the stories about his superhuman status as a demi-god? He is said to have been two-thirds god and one-third human, like the biblical accounts of Nephilim. Were other records of myth potentially the accounts of actual interaction between heroes and men? Hybrids!? As has been and will continue to be discussed throughout this book, biblical and extra-biblical records seem to indicate there might be more to this mythology than myth.

In my second book, *The Gods Who Walk Among Us*, I discuss

the relationship between gods and demigods and the
that were passed down from Sumeria:

> Birds skipped among groves of date palms along the
> marshy banks of the Euphrates in the year 3500 BC.
> As the sun arose above Sumer, the alluvial desert of the
> Middle East came alive with agricultural activity. In a
> valley forged between the twin rivers of the Tigris and
> the Euphrates, magnificent walled cities awoke to the
> chatter of busy streets and marketplaces. In what the
> Greeks would later call "Mesopotamia" (*between the
> rivers*), the world's first great trade center and civiliza-
> tion had developed. The opulent Sumerian cities of
> Ur—the home of Abram—Uruk, and Lagash, had
> become the economic machines of the ancient Middle
> East, and industries from as far away as Jericho, near the
> Mediterranean Sea, and Çatal Hüyük, in Asia Minor,
> competed for the trade opportunities they provided.
> Laborers from the biblical city of Jericho exported salt
> into Sumer, and miners from Çatal Hüyük prepared
> obsidian, used in making mirrors, for shipment into the
> ancient metropolis.
>
> Yet, while the prehistoric people of the East looked
> to the Sumerians for their supply of daily bread, the
> Sumerians themselves gazed heavenward to the early
> rising of Utu (Shamash), the all-providing sun god,
> as he prepared once again to ride across the sky in his
> mule drawn chariot. Utu was not alone among the gods.
> By now the Sumerian pantheon provided the earliest
> known description of organized mythology, consisting
> of a complex system of more than three thousand deities
> and covering nearly every detail of nature and human

enterprise. There were gods of sunshine and rain. There were vegetation gods, fertility gods, river gods, animal gods, and gods of the afterlife. There were the great gods—Enlil (prince of the air), Anu (ruler of the heavens), Enki, (the god of water), and more. Under these great gods existed a second level of deities, including Nanna (the moon god), Utu (the sun god), and Inanna, (the Queen of Heaven).

As the centuries passed, the god and goddess worshipping cities of the Sumerians began to fade away. The flourishing fields of agriculture that provided the underpinnings of the great Sumerian economy were depleted of fertility through over irrigation, and residue of salt buildup appeared to chaff the surface of the land. The city-states of Sumeria: Kish, Ur, Lagash, and Umma, damaged by a millennium of ruthless infighting among the Sumerians, finally succumbed to militant external forces. The barbarian armies of the Elamites (Persians) invaded and destroyed the city of Ur, and Amorites from the West overran the northern province of Sumer and, subsequently, established the hitherto little-known town of Babylon as their capital.

By 1840 BC, Hammurabi, the sixth king of Babylon, conquered the remaining cities of Sumeria and forged northern Mesopotamia and Sumeria into a single nation. Yet, the ultimate demise of the Sumerian people did not vanquish their ideas. Sumerian art, language, literature, and (especially) religion were forever absorbed into the cultures and social academics of the nations surrounding Mesopotamia, including the Hittite nation, the Baby-lonians, and the ancient Assyrians. (Horn and Jones 15, 17)

In addition to the Sumerian's elaborate pantheon, stories of flying discs and tales of the transdimensional gods who flew in them as well as the gateways through which evil and benevolent influences sought entry were passed on to succeeding faiths.

Such gateways, or stargates, were later represented on earth in Assyrian archways built through elaborate construction ceremonies and blessed by names of good omens. Colossal stone creatures stood guard at the gates and palace entries to keep undesirable forces from coming through the portals—important imitative magic thought to represent heavenly ideas. These guardians were often accompanied by carved winged spirits holding magic devices and/or other magic statuettes concealed beneath the floors.

In what some believe to be reference to ancient UFOs, Sumerian engravings on clay cylinders speak in very similar language to the winged discs found throughout Assyrian mythology in association with Ashur, the flying god of war. Ashur is believed to be a later version of Ahura Mazda, the good god of Zoroastrianism, who is opposed by Ahriman. In each case these beings are depicted coming through or descending from the sky on flying discs. Similar stories are repeated in Egyptian hieroglyphs as well as in the literature of Greece and other cultures around the world.

ENTER ATUM

A benefactor of the Sumerian ideas, and a people who would ultimately make their own contributions to the ancient mythologies, was an old and flourishing population of agrarians known as the Egyptians. By the year 1350 BC, Egyptian dominance had spread from Syria and Palestine into the farthest corners of the Fertile Crescent. From northern Mesopotamia to the Baltic Sea, the pharaohs of Egypt had established themselves as the social and economic leaders of the civilized world, ruling an area more than two thousand miles in length. The military superiority of the Egyptian army demonstrated its ability to subdue the threat of resistance, and as a result, allowed the Egyptians to maintain a hegemony that extended from the Nubians to the Hyksos. Yet, in the final analysis, it was the influence of the gods of Egypt—their magic, myths, and rituals—that provided the Egyptians with a lasting place in history and brought following generations into an immense, "enlightening" description of ancient mythology, including a wealth of information regarding the dynamics and supernatural possibilities of pyramids, paganism, and portals.

FIRST ACT OF CREATION: ATUM (RA, THE SUN GOD)

Prehistoric Egyptians held the premise that the oceans preceded and in some way contributed to the creation of the living cosmos. From the Fifth Dynasty Pyramid Texts, the Heliopolitan theory of creation states that Atum (the sun god Ra) independently created himself from a singular expression of self will—an act visualized by the Egyptians as a divine egg that appeared upon the primordial waters of the all-filling ocean called Nun, out of which Atum, "He who created himself," emerged.

Interestingly, Egyptians described Ra as navigating the heavens in a flying "boat." Horus was a descendant of Ra and flew through the heavens on a winged disc as well, which "shined with many colors" (Budge). A hieroglyphic in the temple at Edfu describes one such event:

So Horus, the Winged Measurer, flew up toward the horizon in the Winged Disc of Ra; it is therefore that he has been called from that day on Great God, Lord of the Skies....Then Horus, the Winged Measurer, reappeared in the Winged Disc, which shined in many colors; and he came back to the boat of Ra, the Falcon of the Horizon....And Thoth said: "O Lord of the gods! The Winged Measurer has returned in the great Winged Disc, shining with many colors." (Budge)

SECOND ACT OF CREATION AND A FLYING EYE

According to Egyptian myth, a second act of creation developed around a divine masturbation when Atum, the great "He-She," orally copulated himself and afterward regurgitated his children— Shu and Tefnut—who assumed the positions of god and goddess of air and moisture. Later, when Shu and Tefnut became lost in the universal ocean of Nun, Atum exhibited his paternal care by sending out his Eye, which had the curious habit of detaching itself from Atum and of thinking independent thoughts, to look for them. The flying Eye of Atum found the child gods and eventually returned to discover that Atum had grown impatient during the wait and had created a second eye. In order to placate the hostility that developed between the two divine eyes, Atum affixed the first eye upon his forehead where it was to oversee and rule the world of creation. Thus the Eye of Atum became the jealous, destructive aspect of the sun god Ra.

To avoid getting lost again in the all-filling waters of Nun, Shu and Tefnut procreated Geb (the earth) and Nut (the sky) and thus provided the more stable elements of earth, nature, and the seasons. Later, Geb was conceptualized as cohabiting with Nut and producing four children of his own: Seth, Osiris, Isis, and Nephthys. Of these, Osiris and Isis grew into such important cult deities that the mythology of the Egyptian religion was modified to support the claim that Osiris, with the help of his sister-wife Isis, had nearly overthrown and replaced Ra as the most powerful of the gods—an action that so enraged his brother Seth that the hateful and jealous sibling killed him.

Seth's murderous act was followed by the jackal-headed god, Anubis, assisting Isis with the embalming of her slain husband-brother Osiris, an act through which Anubis secured his position as "the god of embalming." Then, while still in mourning, Isis summoned the wisdom of Thoth, which she combined with her own proficient magical skills, and produced a resurrected Osiris, who, in turn, impregnated her with Horus, the god of daylight. Horus promptly avenged his father's death by killing the evil brother Seth.

Another version of the myth claims that Horus was born to Isis only after she impregnated herself with semen that she had taken from the corpse of Osiris—evidence perhaps of advanced science such as artificial insemination or even cloning. The god Seth was angry and sought to destroy Horus. Note how Isis seeks help from Thoth, who comes in a flying craft—the Boat of the Celestial Disc—as recorded in the Metternich Stela:

> Then Isis sent forth a cry to heaven and addressed her appeal to the Boat of Millions of Years. And the Celestial Disc stood still, and moved not from the place where it was. And Thoth came down, and he was provided with magical powers, and possessed the great power....And he said: "O Isis, thou goddess, thou glorious one,...I have come this day in the Boat of the Celestial Disc from the place where it was yesterday....I have come from the skies to save the child for his mother." (Budge)

Another story claims that Seth persuaded his brother Osiris to climb into a box, which he quickly shut and threw into the Nile. Osiris drowned, and his body floated down the Nile river where it snagged on the limbs of a tamarisk tree. In Byblos, Isis recovered the body from the river bank and took it into her care. In her absence, Seth stole the body again and chopped it into fourteen pieces, which he threw into the Nile. Isis searched the river bank until she recovered every piece, except for the genitals, which had been swallowed by a fish (Plutarch says a crocodile). But Isis simply replaced the missing organ with a facsimile and somehow was able to reconstruct Osiris and impregnate herself with the phallus.

This portion of the Isis/Osiris myth may have been developed over time to provide the legend necessary to sanction the kind of temple prostitution practiced during the rituals of Isis. Temple prostitutes represented the human manifestation of the goddess and were available for ritual sex as a form of imitative magic. Much of the details are no longer available, but it appears these prostitutes usually began their services to the goddess as a child and were deflowered at a very young age by a priest or, as Isis was, by a carved phallus of the god Osiris. Sometimes prostitutes were chosen, on the basis of their beauty, as the mates of sacred temple bulls. Such bulls were considered the incarnation of Osiris, whereas in other places, such as at Mendes, temple prostitutes were offered in coitus to divine goats.

Regardless, from this time forward Osiris was considered the chief god of the deceased and the judge of the netherworld—the dark and dreary underworld region of the dead. In human form Osiris was perceived as a mummy, and, paradoxically, while he was loved as the guarantor of life after death, he was feared as the demonic presence that decayed the bodies of the dead. Such necromantic worship of Osiris and Isis grew to become an important part of several Mediterranean religions, with the most famous cult center of Osiris at Abydos in Upper Egypt, where an annual festival reenacted his death and resurrection. In Abydos, Osiris was called the god of the setting sun—the mysterious "force" that ruled the region of the dead just beneath the western horizon. He was venerated in this way primarily because death, and specifically the fear of one's estate after death, grew to constitute so much of Egyptian concern.

In the funerary texts known as the *Book of the Dead*, the most elaborate magical steps were developed around the Osiris myth to assist the Egyptians with their journey into the afterlife. It was believed that every person had a Ka—a spiritual and invisible duplicate—and that such Ka accompanied him or her throughout eternity. Since the Ka provided each person with a resurrected body in the kingdom of the dead, but could not exist without the maintenance of the earthly body, every effort was made to preserve the human corpse. The body was therefore mummified according to the elaborate magic rituals passed down from Isis, who, according to legend, singularly perfected the rituals of mummification through her work on Osiris. Wooden replicas of the body were also placed in the tomb as a kind of substitute in case the mummy was accidentally destroyed, and additional protection for the corpse was provided through the construction of ingenious burial tombs specifically designed to hide and preserve the human body for all of eternity. Finally, curses were placed throughout the tomb as a warning to intruders.

At death the Egyptian Ka departed from the body and, accompanied by the hymns and prayers of the living, used the formulas memorized from the funerary texts to outsmart the horrible demons seeking to impede the Ka's progress into the kingdom (or hall) of Osiris. Arriving at the judgment hall, the heart of the Ka was "weighed in the balance" by Osiris and his forty-two demons. If the deceased was found lacking in virtue, he was condemned to an eternity of hunger and thirst. If the Ka was determined to have belonged to an outright "sinner," it was cut to pieces and fed to Ammit—the miserable little goddess and "eater of souls." But if the deceased was judged to have lived a virtuous life, the Ka was granted admittance into the heavenly fields of Yaru, where foods were abundant and pleasures unending. The only toil in this heaven was to serve in the grain fields of Osiris, and even this could be obviated by placing substitutionary statues, called Shawabty, into the tomb.

There is some evidence that the forty-two demons or "judges" of Osiris were in some way related to the prehistoric legend of the Watchers. As mentioned in chapter 2, the Egyptian people originally migrated from the biblical land of Shinar, which some say means "the Land of the Watchers." The Egyptians called it *Ta Neter*, The Land of the Watchers "from which the gods came into Egypt." It is possible that a historical event occurred that gave birth to the legend of the Watchers and to the references (attested to by numerous ancient texts) of a race of "watcher/gods" that cohabited with women and that sought to control the human race.

In the Egyptian *Book of the Dead* there are prayers for deliverance from these Watchers who came from Ta-Ur, the "Far Away Land," and in the Book of Jubilees—also known as the Apocalypse of Moses—the Watchers are compared to the "supernatural beings" mentioned in the sixth chapter of Genesis as having come down from heaven to cohabit with women, a union ultimately leading to the birth of the giants. The Apocryphal Book of Enoch also associates the creatures of Genesis 6 with the Watchers, as previously noted in chapter 2.

In either case, whether the Watchers are considered to be from a "far away land" or supernatural beings from heaven, the early Egyptian scribes believed the leaders from among these fallen Watchers had become the underworld demons of Osiris, whose "terrible knives" exacted judgment upon the Ka of the wicked. The Egyptians were desperately afraid of these netherworld "watchers," and a significant amount of time was spent determining how to placate the judgment of Osiris and his forty-two demons. The worship of Isis—the sister-wife of Osiris—thus became integral. As one of the most important goddesses of ancient mythology, Isis was venerated by the Egyptians, Greeks, and the Romans, as the "goddess of a thousand names" and as the undisputed queen of magical skills. Her enchantments were so powerful that she even forced the reluctant sun god Ra to reveal his most secret name. She accomplished this by conjuring a magic serpent that bit the sun god—a reptile whose venom was so potent that it brought Ra to the point of death—thus he surrendered his hidden and powerful name to the goddess. In response, Isis uttered secret words which drove the serpent's poison from Ra's body. Afterward, the victorious goddess celebrated by adding Ra's powerful and hidden name to her archive of divine words.

Isis' magical words were considered by the Egyptians to be of the highest importance for the preparation and navigation of this world and the afterlife. This was because Isis not only possessed secret words, but she instructed her followers as to how, when, and with what vocal tones they were to be uttered. If the proper words were pronounced perfectly—at the right time of the day and with the proper ceremony—they would have the effect of altering reality, manipulating the laws of physics, and of forcing the being or object to which they were directed into compliance, including evil spirits.

An example of this form of magic is found in the "Theban

Recension" of the *Book of the Dead* and depicts Isis as providing a spell for controlling the forty-two demons of Osiris. The formula consists of an amulet made of carnelian that has been soaked in the water of ankhami flowers. The amulet is supposed to be placed around the neck of the dead person in combination with the spoken words of magic. If performed properly, it would empower the Ka of the individual to enter into the region of the dead under the protection of Isis, where the Ka would thereafter move about wheresoever it wanted without fear of the forty-two demons of Osiris.

The only Egyptian who did not benefit from this particular spell was Pharaoh and for a very good reason. Although Pharaoh was considered the son of the sun god Ra and the incarnation of the falcon god Horus during life, in death he became Osiris—judge of the netherworld. On earth, Pharaoh's son and predecessor would take his place as the newly anointed manifestation of Horus—the divine son of Ra and earthly representative of the supreme god of cosmic deities, in short, god on earth. Thus, each new generation of pharaohs provided the "gods" with a spokesman for the present world and for the afterlife.

AN INTERESTING QUESTION
ABOUT PHARAOHS AND GODS

While conducting a recent tour of Egypt and the Holy Land, my good friend and recipient of the DAR "Historian of the Year" award, Dr. Donald C. Jones, stood outside the Great Pyramid in Giza and pondered such knowledge and where it had been derived. Who among the ancients would have been capable of building a single structure over thirty times larger than the Empire State Building? By the most conservative

figures, the Great Pyramid was built over 4,500 years ago (many
.believe 12,000 years or longer) and out of more than 2 million
blocks of stone weighing between two and sixty tons each. It was
also constructed by builders whose knowledge of the earth and
of planetary systems was so advanced that the Great Pyramid
faces true North, South, East, and West while also standing at
the exact center of the Earth's land mass and at a height exactly
that of the earth's mean sea level. One would hypothesize that
the leader of such a people would have indeed been perceived
by ancients as a god on earth. Whereas many scholars believe
the Great Pyramid—the last standing monument of the Seven
Wonders of the Ancient World—was built around the year 2560
BC by Khufu (Cheops), the Pharaoh of the Fourth Egyptian
Dynasty, others disagree. These dissenters' mysterious reasons will
be introduced in chapter 4 as the gods of Greece are examined.

Chapter 4

FALLEN ANGELS: ANCIENT MYTHOLOGY

Not long ago a man whom I have come to know as a friend wrote a book called *The Nephilim and the Pyramid of the Apocalypse.* Patrick Heron published his study after delving into the history of the pyramids, seeking to explain who built the structures, how they acquired such mathematical and astronomical knowledge, and what advanced technology was used in the construction. The answer he came up with was astonishing: the pyramids were built by the Nephilim.

After reading Heron's explanations, I pointed out to him that the prophet Isaiah was most probably discussing the Great Pyramid of Giza when he prophesied, "In that day shall there be an altar to the Lord in the midst of the land of Egypt, and a pillar at the border thereof to the Lord. And it shall be for a sign and for a witness unto the Lord of hosts in the land of Egypt" (Is. 19.19-21a). The Great Pyramid was the only "pillar" standing on the old border dividing Lower and Upper Egypt in Isaiah's day, but why would the prophet point to it as a Last Days sign unto the Lord? Patrick answered me with the "shape" of things to come. He believes New Jerusalem is pyramidal, as opposed to cubic in shape, and that Watchers conveyed this design to the Nephilim following what they had seen in heaven.

...AND THEN CAME THE GREEKS

Like Egyptian heritage, the Greeks may teach us something of what was learned from Watchers and their offspring. The Greeks began with the Dorians who came out of the north by the tens of thousands. They were nearly invincible Indo-European invaders riding in horse-drawn chariots of war. Between 2800 and 2000 BC, they conquered most of the indigenous inhabitants of the Middle East—from the inland people of Asia Minor to the Macedonians and beyond—and they did it in the name of their sky god, the thunderous and fearsome Zeus. The Dorian mix of Sumerian legend included Mycenaean and Minoan interpretations as well, blending numerous religious concepts into an influential society of gods eventually known as the Olympians. As the famous (and sometimes infamous) gods of Greece came to dwell above the towering Mount Olympus in the north, the gods took various roles under Zeus, including Hera, Poseidon, Hades, Demeter, Apollo, Artemis, Ares, Aphrodite, Hermes, Athena, Hephaestus, and Hestia (later replaced by Dionysus). A complex system of lesser deities developed beneath these principle gods including Adonis, Selene, Hypnos, Asclepius, Eros, and Hercules.

We find particular interest in the character of the king of the gods, Zeus. There was scarcely any part of Greek life in which Zeus was not involved. He was Zeus Herkeios, "Protector of the House" and Zeus Ktesios, "the Acquirer." He was Zeus

Hikesios, "Friend of the Fugitive" and Zeus Polieus, "Guardian of the City." His firmly held position as the supreme and high god within Greek religion was easily verified by archaeology, not the least of which was the discovery of the great temple of Zeus, a masterwork that stood in the southern part of the precinct of Zeus at Olympia in the Altis forest and exhibited the famous gold and ivory colossus of Zeus by Pheidias (destroyed in AD 462), a masterpiece estimated to have been the greatest work of art in all of antiquity and one of the Seven Wonders of the ancient world.

In addition to being the king of the gods, Zeus was a powerful presence in everyday cult and ritual. His principle oracle stood at Dodona—the chief city of Epirus and the "land of the oak trees"—where a shrine to Zeus had existed since the second millennium BC. For a while the Dodona oracle even rivaled Apollo's famous one at Delphi. At Dodona, Zeus provided inquiring mortals with divine guidance by whispering through the leaves of sacred oak trees attended to by bare-footed priests called Selloi. At other times Zeus communicated through the splashing of water in a nearby sacred spring, or through the cooing of sacred pigeons. Eventually, he simplified his answers, and worshippers cast lots or interpreted the echoes of a gong to receive his divination. But it was the oak tree oracle at Dodona that claimed to be the oldest in Greece and the "father of gods and men." The connection between Zeus and the tree oracles probably began with certain prehistoric religious ideas from Crete and undoubtedly refers to the earliest marriage of the Dorian Zeus and the Minoan/Cretan willow goddesses. In the ancient Minoan settlement of Hagia Triada, Zeus was called Zeus Welkhanos, which means the "god of the willow tree." He was also known by the name Welkhanos at Gortyna and at Phaistos where he was somehow ritually associated with his lover

Leto. The cult worship of Zeus and Leto in Phaistos was curious in its own right because it connected the ancient elements of earth worship (the children of Gaia conversing through various nature manifestations, i.e., the willow tree) and transsexualism. In fact, the worship of Zeus was sometimes overshadowed in Phaistos by the cult of Leto as the Cretan youths cast off their boyish garments during their initiation into manhood. The festival was called the Ekdysai, "casting off" and was associated with the myth of Leucippus—a peculiar legend in which a baby girl, Leucippus, was born to a woman named Galatea who preferred instead to have a son, and so she persuaded Leto to let the girl change her sex into that of a boy when she grew up. During the Cretan initiation the young men lay down beside a statue of Leucippus in the temple of Leto where the blessings of growth and fertility could be invoked.

In Pergamum, perpetual sacrifices were offered to Zeus upon his towering and famous forty-foot high altar—the same artifact that now stands inside the Berlin Museum. Some scholars believe St. Antipas, the first leader and martyr of the early Christian church in Pergamum, was slain for resisting this altar worship of Zeus. Tradition holds that St. Antipas was slowly roasted to death inside the statue of a bull—the symbol and companion of Zeus—and some claim that the passage in Revelation 2.13 is a reference to the cult worship of Zeus at Pergamum: "I know thy works, and where thou dwellest, even where Satan's seat is…wherein Antipas was my faithful martyr, who was slain among you, where Satan dwelleth" (Rev. 2.13). Others believe this passage refers to Caesar worship, while others contend the phrase in Revelation 2.13 is a reference to the cult worship of Asclepius, the Greek god of healing.

Nonetheless, the argument could be made for a Pergamum connection between Zeus and the biblical Satan, as both were considered descending gods of thunder—Zeus in antiquity and Satan in modern times. Zeus was also known as the king or "prince" of the air, as was Satan (Eph. 2.2). Altars were discovered near Pergamum dedicated to Zeus Kataibates, which most accurately means "Zeus who descends," reminiscent of Jesus who said, "I beheld Satan as lightning fall [descend] from heaven" (Luke 10.18).

The references of "Zeus who descends" and the opinion of this as testimony to Lucifer's fall are interesting when one contemplates the next logical question: Where did Lucifer fall from? Some suggest the original domain of Lucifer was among the celestial bodies and that he literally fell "from the heavens." We fictionalize this belief in our novel, *The Ahriman Gate*:

As it turned out, Renaldo believed Ezekiel's citation of Lucifer moving "up and down amidst the stones of fire" was a reference to the once-glorious being's dominion of the planetary belt, including Mars. He had long thought the Cydonia Face and pyramidal structures near it were curious, potentially illustrating a past Martian civilization that, if proven, would provide physical support for the Bible's account of prehistoric war and the subsequent expulsion of Lucifer and his angels "from the heavens."

"Keep in mind," Renaldo shared over the phone, "Such evidence might also provide background for the building of the pyramids and similar structures on Earth—those monuments whose technical requirements seem far in advance of ancient man's comprehension, the physical construction of which may predate Adam and Eve. The astronomical features built into the Great Pyramid alone are startling: how the four corners face true north, south, east, and west; how the antechamber points to the center of the universe; and so on."

Jones, a history scholar in his own right, was fully aware of the pyramid's enigmas, yet now as he listened, he learned something he didn't know.

"Close to the Cydonia Face on Mars is a similar five-sided pyramid with detailed buttressing suspiciously positioned at 1/360th of the Martian polar diameter from the Face. In the same area, other structures form a perfect equilateral triangle in what some experts at NASA are now calling 'the city complex.'"

Copiously scribbling the Bishop's thoughts as he spoke, Jones said, "I wasn't aware of the city complex, but the qualities of the enormous face are astonishing. Eyebrows over eye sockets with pupils. A parted mouth with lips and teeth. A nose tapered back toward the forehead. A crown strikingly similar to those worn by Egyptian and Mayan royalty." Jones had done his homework before calling the scholar.

Renaldo agreed. "Indeed. Mathematicians have postulated the chances of the face arising by chance at a thousand billion, billion to one, so it is significant."

"Significant enough to convince you it's real?" Jones had asked.

"In my opinion, if what we are seeing in NASA's photos represent intelligent engineering, not a trick of shadows and light, we may have no other alternative."

"But isn't that anathema? A challenge to biblical history?"

Clearing his throat, Renaldo had said, "Not really. In fact the answer to this riddle is found in the Bible, I'm sure of it, in such places as the book of Job, where the old prophet tells us that God destroyed the literal dwelling places of the angels that made insurrection against Him. Job specifically mentions the destruction of Rahab, a planetary body also known as 'Pride,' from which God drove 'the fugitive snake.'"

"So you believe, tenuously I take it, that cities on Mars might actually have existed, and that these were abandoned during a pre-Genesis war between Good and Evil?"

"I'd go a step further. If pyramids on Mars are confirmed in my lifetime, disclosed by reputable governments and scientific institutions, mind you, I'll present it to the Vatican as possible proof of such a war."

Jones considered the far-reaching ramifications of that comment, then reiterated, "Not to belabor the point, but wouldn't questions about the central doctrines of Christianity arise during such a discovery? Especially if the Martian buildings match the architecture of structures in Egypt?"

"Satan will use it to his benefit, undoubtedly," Renaldo confirmed. "People will point to Mars and then to the Egyptian desert and say, 'See! Here's proof! We came from aliens! The Bible is a hoax!' This could even be part of the strong delusion prophesied for the End Times."

Having agreed with this and other assessments made by the Bishop, Jones hung up and painstakingly reconstructed each element of the conversation before drawing his own conclusions. (Horn 109-111)

Though fiction, the above dialogue is based on accepted theology concerning Lucifer and the possibility that the location from which he fell was a star system or planetoid. Later on

The Ahriman Gate we dramatize Mars as having become a prison planet, in which the rebel angels are bound. This is fascinating in light of Hesiod's *Theogony*, which describes the place of imprisonment of the Titans:

> And there, all in their order, are the sources and ends of gloomy earth and misty Tartarus and the unfruitful sea and starry heaven, loathsome and dank, which even the gods abhor.
>
> It is a great gulf, and if once a man were within the gates....There stands the awful home of murky Night wrapped in dark clouds. In front of it the son of Iapetus stands immovably upholding the wide heaven upon his head and unwearying hands, where Night and Day draw near and greet one another as they pass the great threshold of bronze....And there the children of dark Night have their dwellings, Sleep and Death, awful gods. The glowing Sun never looks upon them with his beams, neither as he goes up into heaven, nor as he comes down from heaven....(Lines 736-744)

Hesiod's *Theogony* takes on additional mysteries when one considers that the Bible characterizes the place of imprisoned rebel angels using the same words Hesiod employs to describe the place of Titan gods—"Tartarus" and the "Bottomless Pit" (see 2 Peter 2.4; Revelation 9.1-11; 11.7; 17.8; 20.1-3). Couple this with eerily similar discoveries on the actual moon Iapetus, and you understand why a growing number of researchers are open to the possibility that synthetic looking planetoids such as Iapetus are, as it appears to be, artificial.

In Greek mythology Iapetus was the son of Uranus and Gaia, and father of Atlas, Prometheus, Epimetheus, and Menoetius.

Because Atlas was a "father of mankind," Iapetus was understood in myth to be a progenitor, a creator god, of Homo sapiens.

Italian astronomer and engineer Giovanni Domenico Cassini discovered Saturn's moon Iapetus in 1672 using his small refracting telescope. Cassini correctly deciphered the disappearing and reappearing act of Iapetus as due to the moon synchronously rotating with one hemisphere continuously facing Saturn. Iapetus is also divided by a great gulf formed by a giant walled threshold at its equator as seen in the picture of Iapetus on the back cover of this book. This feature was discovered during a New Year's Eve flyby in 2005 when NASA's Cassini spacecraft photographed the 1300 kilometers (808 miles) long and 20 kilometers (12 miles) high rim stretching over one third of the moon's equator. No other moon in the solar system has been found with such a stunning feature: literally a 60,000 foot high wall. Compare this fact again with Hesiod's description of a great threshold of bronze:

It is a great gulf....murky Night wrapped in dark clouds. In front of it the son of Iapetus...where Night and Day draw near and greet one another as they pass the great threshold of bronze....And there the children of dark Night have their dwellings, Sleep and Death, awful gods. The glowing Sun never looks upon them with his beams, neither as he goes up into heaven, nor as he comes down from heaven. (Lines 736-744)

In *The Search for Life in the Universe,* Tobias Owen, the man at NASA who discovered the face on Mars, and Donald Goldsmith wrote that, "This unusual moon [Iapetus] is the only object in the Solar System which we might seriously regard as an alien signpost—a natural object deliberately modified by an advanced civilization to attract our attention...."

(Hoagland). Former NASA consultant Richard Hoagland also raises a number of significant questions about artificiality on Iapetus. Some of Hoagland's comments question how science fiction writer Arthur C. Clarke could have written about these mysteries before they were discovered and why Clarke included a monolith stargate, through which creator beings had passed for millions of years.

In a recent email to me, David Flynn made an interesting point about this including the possibility of the "bottomless pit" (mentioned above) actually being a "star" (or an extraterrestrial object) in heaven:

> Tom, you are intrepid enough to address an issue many are afraid to investigate....And you are right about gates [and that various beings have come through them]....
>
> [Flynn then quotes from Revelation 9] "And he opened the bottomless pit....And there came out of the smoke locusts upon the earth....and the shapes of the locusts [were] like unto horses prepared unto battle; and... their faces [were] as the faces of men. And they had hair of women, and their teeth were as of lions..." (Rev.9.1-8)
>
> [Flynn continues] Here is described an army of beings with mixed genetics [transgenics], but all species of terrestrial origin. The similarities between the "locusts with faces of men" and the modern reports of "insectoid" aliens [descending through dimensional gates] stand out in John's prophecy....It is assumed that the locusts of Revelation 9 "ascend" from a bottomless pit somewhere on earth because the story of the locust invasion begins with a "star" falling from heaven to earth and an angel with a key. The Greek word translated "fall" is *Pipto*,

which means to "descend from a higher place to a lower." If the star itself IS the bottomless pit, Revelation 9 could be describing an extraterrestrial object—a mother ship—moving into orbit around earth with myriad beings. From this same place in Scripture the word "bottomless" is *bathos*, often translated as "height" and the word "pit" is *Phrear*. A phrear in Greek mythology is an orcus, a deep chasm bound by a gulf where fallen beings are imprisoned….Revelation 12 explains the surety of Satan and his angels coming down from heaven to the earth in the future. For now, they wait…somewhere out in space. (Flynn 2005)

David Flynn's study on this was published in his book *Cydonia: The Secret Chronicles of Mars*. One can easily imagine, if Flynn is correct, how Official Disclosure would be forced on the world by a sudden, inexplicable movement of an extra solar planetoid and the human hysteria that would follow if Iapetus or a similar "moon" unexpectedly turned and headed toward earth!

BACK TO THE FUTURE

It was discussed in the second chapter of this book that scholars accept the idea that planetoids—at least the physical earth—can contain extra-dimensional ("spiritual") entities locked away or contained behind barriers of some type—as in gates—with warnings to humans about seeking their communion. When contact has been desired, beings of startling similarity have materialized from sky, sea, or beneath the earth's surface, as they did in the biblical narrative of 1 Samuel, where they ascended from "out of the earth" and were interpreted as gods. I mentioned modern examples in chapter 2 including a being that is strikingly similar to an alien Grey in Aleister Crowley's "Amalantrah Working" ritual and the subsequent "Babalon Working" ritual by Crowley's students Jack Parsons and L. Ron Hubbard, who sought to incarnate the spirit of Babylon.

ANCIENT GREEKS BROUGHT "GODS" THROUGH IN SIMILAR WAYS

Dionysus, the thirteenth god of the Greeks, was the divine son of Zeus and of the mortal Semele. He was often depicted as the inventor of wine, abandon, and revelry, but this description seems inadequate in that it refers only to the basic elements of intoxication and enthusiasm that were used by the Bacchae (female participants of the Dionystic mysteries, also known as Maenads and Bacchantes) in their rituals to incarnate Dionysus. Followers of Dionysus believed he was the "presence," otherwise defined as the craving, within man that longs to "let itself go" and to "give itself over" to baser earthly desires. What some might resist as the lustful wants of the carnal man, followers of Dionysus embraced as the incarnation of power that would, in the next life, liberate the souls of men from the constraints of the present world and from the customs that sought to define respectability through obedience to moral law. Until that day arrived, worshippers of Dionysus attempted to bring themselves into union with the god through a ritual casting off of the bonds of sexual denial and primal constraint by inviting him to enter them via a state of ecstasy.

According to myth, the uninhibited rituals of *ecstasy*, Greek for "outside the body," brought followers of Dionysus into a supernatural condition that enabled them to escape the temporary limitations of body and mind and to achieve a state of *enthousiasmos,* or "inside the god." In this sense Dionysus represented a dimensional dichotomy within Greek religion, as the primary maxim of the Greek culture was of moderation or "nothing too extreme." Yet Dionysus embodied the absolute extreme in that he sought to inflame the forbidden passions of human desire.

Interestingly, as most students of psychology will understand, this gave Dionysus a stronger allure among Greeks who otherwise tried in so many ways to suppress and control the wild and secret lusts of the human heart. Dionysus resisted every such effort and, according to myth, visited a terrible madness upon those who denied him free expression. The Dionystic idea of mental disease resulting from suppression of inner desire, especially aberrant sexual desire, was later reflected in teachings of Sigmund Freud. Thus Freudianism might be called the grandchild of the cult of Dionysus.

Conversely, the person who gave himself over to the will of Dionysus was rewarded with unlimited psychological and physical delights. Such mythical systems of mental punishments and physical rewards based on resistance and/or submission to Dionysus were both symbolically and literally illustrated in the cult rituals of the Bacchae. The Bacchae women (married and unmarried Greek women who had the right to participate in the mysteries of Dionysus) migrated in frenzied hillside groups, dressed transvestite in fawn skins, and were accompanied by screaming, music, dancing, and licentious behavior. When, for instance, a baby animal was too young and lacking in instinct to sense the danger and run away from the revelers, it was picked up and suckled by nursing mothers who participated in the hillside rituals. However, when older animals sought to escape the marauding Bacchae, they were considered "resistant" to the will of Dionysus and were torn apart and eaten alive as part of the fevered ritual. Human participants were sometimes subjected to the same orgiastic cruelty, as the rule of the cult was "anything goes." Later versions of the ritual of Bacchanalia became so debauched that eventually it was outlawed. Until then, any creature that dared to resist such perversion of Dionysus was often subjected to *sparagmos*, "torn apart" and *omophagia*, "consumed raw."

In 410 BC, Euripides wrote of the bloody rituals of the Bacchae in his famous play, *The Bacchantes*:

> …the Bacchantes…with hands that bore no weapon of steel, attacked our cattle as they browsed. Then wouldst thou have seen Agave mastering some sleek lowing calf, while others rent the heifers limb from limb. Before thy eyes there would have been hurling of ribs and hoofs this way and that, and strips of flesh, all blood be-dabbled, dripped as they hung from the pine branches. Wild bulls, that glared but now with rage along their horns, found themselves tripped up, dragged down to earth by countless maidens hands.

Euripedes goes on to describe how Pentheus, King of Thebes, was torn apart and eaten alive by his own mother as, according to the play, she fell under the spell of Dionysus.

The tearing apart and eating alive of a sacrificial victim refers to the earliest history of Dionysus. Ancient and violent cult rituals existing since the dawn of paganism stipulated that by eating alive or by drinking the blood of an enemy or an animal a person might capture the essence or "soul-strength" of the victim. The earliest Norwegian huntsmen believed this idea, and they drank the blood of bears in effort to capture their physical strength. East African Masai warriors also practiced omophagia, and they sought to gain the strength of the wild by drinking the blood of lions. Human victims were treated in this way by head-hunters of the East Indies in an effort to capture their essence.

Today, omophagia is practiced by certain Voodoo sects as well as by cult Satanists. I must point out that eating human flesh and drinking human blood as an attempt to "become one" with the devoured is today, in many cases, a demonization of the Eucharist, or Holy Communion. Yet sparagmos and omophagia, as practiced by followers of Dionysus, was not an attempt of transubstantiation as in the Catholic Eucharist nor of consubstantiation as in the Lutheran communion nor of a symbolic ordinance as in the fundamentalist denomination, which all include the common goal of elevating the worshipper into sacramental communion with God. The goal of the Bacchae was the opposite: the frenzied dance, the thunderous song, the licentious behavior, the tearing apart and eating alive, all were efforts on the part of the Bacchae to capture the essence of the god Dionysus and to bring him through the portal into an incarnated rage within humans. The idea was more of possession by Dionysus then communion.

Hebrews believed demonic possession actually occurred during the mystery rituals of Dionysus. They considered Hades, the Greek god of the underworld, to be equal with Hell and/or the Devil, and many ancient writers likewise saw no difference between Hades, in this sense the Devil, and Dionysus. Euripedes echoed this sentiment in the *Hecuba*, and referred to the followers of Dionysus as the "Bacchants of Hades." In Syracuse, Dionysus was known as *Dionysus Morychos*, "the dark one," a fiendish creature roughly equivalent to the biblical Satan, who wore goatskins and dwelt in the region of the underworld.

In the scholarly book, *Dionysus: Myth And Cult*, Walter F. Otto connects Dionysus with the prince of the underworld:

The similarity and relationship which Dionysus has with the prince of the underworld (and this is revealed by a large number of comparisons) is not only confirmed by an authority of the first rank, but he says the two deities are actually the same. Heraclitus says, "...Hades and Dionysus, for whom they go mad and rage, are one and the same" (116)

Yet, the Hebrews considered the magic ceremonies of the Bacchae to be the best evidence of Dionysus' "Satanic" connection. While most details are no longer available because Dionysus was a mystery god and his rituals were thus revealed to the initiated only, the Hebrew prophet Ezekiel describes the "magic bands," *kesatot*, of the Bacchae, which, as in the omophagia, were used to capture, or magically imprison, the souls of men:

> Therefore, thus says the Lord GOD, "Behold I am against your magic bands [kesatot] by which you hunt lives [souls] there as birds, and I will tear them off your arms; and I will let them go, even those lives [souls] whom you hunt as birds" (NAS, Ezek. 13.20)

Acts 17 gives an account of a man who may have been similarly liberated from control of Dionysus: "Howbeit certain men clave unto [Paul], and believed: among the which was Dionysius the Areopagite" (KJV, Acts 17.34). To carry the name of Dionysus typically meant one of two things: 1) the parents were devotees of Dionysus and thus the child was "predestined" to be a follower of the god, or 2) the individual was under the spell of the *kesatot*. The *kesatot* was a magic arm band used in connection with an *orca*, or container, called the *kiste*. Wherever the kiste is inscribed on sarcophagi and on Bacchic scenes, it is depicted as a sacred vessel (a soul prison?) with a snake peering through an open lid. How the magic worked and in what way a soul was imprisoned is still a mystery. Pan, the half-man/half-goat god, later relegated to devildom, is sometimes pictured as kicking the lid open and letting the snakes (souls?) out. Such loose snakes were then depicted as being enslaved around the limbs, and bound in the hair, of the Bacchae women.

Such images of Pan, the serpents, the imprisoned souls, and the magic *Kesatot* and *Kiste*, have never been adequately explained by available authorities, and the interpretation of this imagery as showing a method for imprisoning souls is thus subject to ongoing scrutiny.

Yet, since the prophet Ezekiel spoke of the efforts of the Bacchae to imprison the souls of men mystically through the magic bands of Dionysus, and since Pan was most beloved of Dionysus because of his *pandemonium*, "all the devils," which struck sudden panic in the hearts of men and beasts, and since the serpent was universally accepted by the Hebrews as a symbol of occult devotion, it can be easily surmised that the iconography of Dionysus represents tenacious effort on the part of the Bacchae to employ symbolic and imitative magic—based on deeply held ancient beliefs about orcas and containers—to incarnate the god through dimensional openings.

Chapter 5

THE COMMON THREAD

C hapter 4 and chapter 1 discussed Dionysus' and Demeter's mystery religions and the association with ceremony and ritual involving imitative magic based on universal beliefs about spirit-containers, orcas, and pits. The importance of such beliefs is found in the broader context of spirit beings held within or behind "gated" areas of inner earth, sea, and sky, as is also reflected in the Bible. While much is still unknown about the mysteries of these deities, the basis of Demeter's popularity was almost certainly rooted in her divinity as a mother-earth goddess. Demeter actually means "earth mother" (*De* or Da "earth" and *meter* "mother"). As mother earth, Demeter was the giver of generosity and grace and the controller of the awesome forces of nature. She was loved as the giver of food and fertility and feared as the taker of life. She could open her womb with blessings and abundance or enclose the dead in her soil.

Without a doubt, the worship of the earth's "spirit" as a mother and the incarnation of the earth's fertility forces within specific goddesses was one of the oldest and most widely held religious ideas in antiquity. Whether it was Inanna of the Sumerians, Ishtar of the Babylonians, or Fortuna of the Romans, every civilization had a sect based on the embodiment of the earth's spirit as a mother-goddess. The Egyptians worshipped Hathor in this way, as did the Chinese, Shingmoo. The Germans worshipped Hertha as the great Mother Earth, and even some Hebrews idolized "the queen of heaven." In Greece, the queen of the Olympian goddesses and wife of Zeus was Hera, the benevolent earth mother. Before her was Gaia (*Gaea*, the Greek creator-mother earth) and beneath her many others including Artemis, Aphrodite, and Hecate.

The principle idea was that the earth is a living entity. The ancient and universally accepted notion that the "living earth" was also a fertile mother was conceptualized in different ways and in various goddess myths and images throughout the ancient world. In *The Golden Ass*, by second century Roman philosopher Lucius Apuleius, the earth was perceived as a feminine force, which incarnated itself at various times and to different people within the goddess mothers. Note how Lucius, a character of the novel, prays to the earth spirit:

> O blessed Queene of Heaven, whether thou be the Dame Ceres [Demeter] which art the original and motherly source of all fruitful things in earth, who after the finding of thy daughter Proserpina [Persephone], through thy great joy which thou diddest presently conceive, madest barraine and unfruitful ground to be plowed and sowne, and now thou inhabitest in the land of Eleusie [Eleusis]; or whether thou be the celestial Venus....[or] horrible Proserpina thou hast the power to stoppe and put away the invasion of the hags and

ghoasts which appeare unto men, and to keep them
downe in the closures [womb] of the earth; thou which
nourishest all the fruits of the world by thy vigor and
force; with whatsoever name is or fashion it is lawful to
call upon thee, I pray thee, to end my great travaile...

The earth spirit responds to Lucius:

Behold Lucius I am come, thy weeping and prayers hath
mooved me to succour thee. I am she that is the natural
mother of all things, mistresse and governesse of all the
elements, the initial progeny of worlds, chiefe of powers divine, Queene of heaven, the principal of the Gods
celestial, the light of the goddesses: at my will the planets
of the ayre [air], the wholesome winds of the Seas, and
the silence of hell be disposed; my name, my divinity
is adored throughout all the world in divers manners,
in variable customes and in many names, for the Phry-
gians call me the mother of the Gods: the Athenians,
Minerva: the Cyprians, Venus: the Candians, Diana:
the Sicilians, Proserpina: the Eleusians, Ceres: some
Juno, other Bellona, other Hecate: and principally the
aethiopians...Queene Isis. (Book Eleven 1566)

Some assume, based on such texts, that a single spiritual
source or realm energized the many goddess myths. In the
ancient hymn, "To Earth the Mother of All," Homer illustrates
how the earth-spirit was universally involved in the affairs and
lives of nations. Through Homer's dedication to the earth, one
discovers how far-reaching and omnipresent the mother-earth
spirit was thought to be:

I will sing of well founded Earth, mother of all, eldest of all beings. She feeds all creatures that are in the world, all that go upon the goodly land, and all that are in the paths of the seas, and all that fly: all these are fed by her store. Through you, O queen, men are blessed in their children and blessed in their harvests, and to you it belongs to give means of life to mortal men and to take it away. Happy is the man whom you delight to honour! He hath all things abundantly: his fruitful land is laden with corn, his pastures are covered with cattle, and his house is filled with good things. Such men rule orderly in their cities of fair women: great riches and wealth follow them: their sons exult with ever-fresh delight, and their daughters in flower-laden bands play and skip merrily over the soft flowers of the field. Thus it is with those whom you honour O holy goddess, bountiful spirit. Hail, mother of the gods, wife of starry Heaven; freely bestow upon me for this my song substance that cheers the heart! And now I will remember you and another song also. (*The Hymns of Homer*, XXX, Chapter 11:1-19)

From these and other ancient records it is obvious that the earth spirit was more than an agricultural or herbaceous facility, *she* was the personable and "eldest of all beings," the "holy goddess," the "bountiful spirit," the all nourishing mother of men who manifested herself within the popular idols of the many goddess myths.

Christian theologians agree that the physical earth contains living, spiritual forces. As previously noted in chapter 1 of this book, Scripture supports such an assertion. The book of Revelation references "the four angels which are bound in the great river Euphrates" (Rev. 9.14). Likewise, Job states that "Dead things are formed from under the waters" (Job 26.5). The literal Hebrew translation of Job 26.5 is, "The Rafa [fallen angels] are made to writhe from beneath the waters." Additional biblical references such as 2 Pet. 2.4 and Jude 6 typify the earth as a kind of holding tank, or prison, where God has bound certain fallen entities. That such fallen spirits seek to communicate with, or participate in, the affairs of humanity, is also defined in Scripture. For example, the Hebrews were warned of spirits that might seek regular communion with men (Deut. 18.11), and when the witch of Endor communicated with these spirits, they ascended up from "out of the earth" (1 Sam. 28.13) as "gods".

Based on the above cited texts, it appears the dynamic (or energy) behind the earth-goddess-spirits was, at least by perception, real. According to the Christian doctrine, this force is identical with legions of fallen spiritual forces bound within the earth, sea, and heavens. Such general conclusions are also made due to the description of biblical demons within the body of the earth, the nature of the manifestations, or attributes, of the gods and goddesses, and the earth-goddess-mothers Isis, Demeter, Persephone, and others who were openly connected with "evil spirits" of the underworld by ancient Hebrews.

STARGATES OF THE GODS

Among the legends of these imprisoned spirit beings, methodology existed whereby they could at least in some cases transcend the barriers that held them. In one example (we shall consider other examples later), Greco-Babylonian astrology and Hermeticism (which passed into Gnostic Christianity though later was rejected by the official church as heresy) included forms of alchemy or magic having the perceived ability to move these "spirits" from behind gateways through statues, persons, or flying winged-discs along heavenly (sky) locations.

In Hermetic iconography, the beginning and ending points of the sky are positioned where the ecliptic, the pathway of the sun, crosses the Milky Way. Universal descriptions depict the distance between these points as a snake called *ouroboros* (or, in Latinized form, *uroborus* or in Greek ό), the "tail-devourer," encompassing the heavens and swallowing its tail. This is one of the oldest mystical symbols in the world and can be found in Aztec, Chinese, and Native American mythologies, among others. In alchemical symbolism, the mouth of the snake is viewed as a place of arrival and departure of "spirit beings" (gods, angels, higher self) who use wormholes, or in my opinion, "stargates," to navigate dimensions or heaven; for example, the god Quetzalcoatl, the most vicious and well-known Aztec deity (important throughout Mesoamerica for nearly 2000 years, from 2500 BC until the Spanish Conquest) connected to the planet Venus is portrayed as "being" or "entering" the ouroboros on Aztec and Toltec ruins. In some renderings a ladder is seen descending from the ecliptic—such as when Quetzalcoatl descends from the sky on a rope ladder or when Jacob in the Bible sees a ladder leading up into heaven—providing a connecting point between earth and heaven. (Early Christians were familiar with teachings about "Gates of Heaven," and some suggest St. Peter's appointment as "gate-keeper" is a reference to this belief. Statues of Peter often show him holding two keys—the keys to lower and higher heaven, life and death, heaven and hell, or other dualisms. Some believe that Jesus Himself referred to these gates in Matthew 7.14 and 16.18.)

One of the recently compelling aspects of the universal serpent-stargate imagery has to do with the year 2012 and the prophesied "end of times" reopening of the serpent portal. The end of the great cycle of the Maya calendar and the planetary cycle of the Aztec calendar is December 21, 2012. According to *The Bible Code*, the world will end on this date due to a collision with a meteor, asteroid, or comet. Another theory—the "Novelty Theory"—claims time itself is a "fractal wave," which will end abruptly in 2012. Even the popular television program *X-Files* speculated that colonization of the earth by "aliens" would occur in December 2012.

Yet, the Maya have a different theory. They describe past visits of Quetzalcoatl, the Feathered Serpent (according to some, "feathered" equates to flying technology while "serpent" refers to the heavenly wormhole-stargate), descending through a "hole in the sky" on a rope ladder (another version of the descending-Quetzalcoatl myth describes him sailing down on a winged ship). They prophecy in 2012 this "serpent rope" will emerge again from the center of the Milky Way, and Quetzalcoatl will return.

David Flynn, author of Cydonia: The Secret Chronicles of Mars, emailed me in 2005 to say:

> Tom, in the zodiac, where the sun travels across the sky, the four brightest stars are found four signs apart in Taurus, Leo, Aquarius, and Scorpio (Ophiuchus). This is where things get interesting: only two of these signs, the bull and Scorpio, occupy the places where the Milky Way crosses the ecliptic. At Scorpio the ecliptic crosses the Milky Way at galactic center. Scorpio is only part of the full sign that is most corrupted of the ancient zodiac symbols. It has been purposely obscured. In ancient times it was a composite sign of both an eagle and a serpent, ergo Ophiuchus (the serpent holder). Both these symbols were assigned to the

tribe of Dan. Every 6,480 years these signs align with the cardinal points of the year, the solstices and the equinoxes [the precession of the equinoxes is divided into four distinct ages of 6,480 years or 25,920 (the zodiacal cycle) divided by 4. The zodiacal cycle, which lasts 25,920 years, has four fixed signs—Aquarius, Taurus, Leo and Scorpio—separated by 6,480 years each. Note in the Bible that we see an angel with four faces—the face of a Lion (Leo), a Bull (Taurus), a Man (the angel) and an Eagle (Ophiuchus)]. It is at this time that the faces of the cherubim are aligned with the divisions of the year that the old age dies and the new age begins. Particularly with the sign of Dan at galactic center, the indication of the end of the age is most dramatic. On the morning when the sun rises in this sign, also at the galactic center, the Milky Way surrounds the horizon of the earth. Ophiuchus is perched atop the galactic bulge with the sun rising at its feet....

The complete symbol of the 33rd degree Mason comprises all the factors of the timing of this event....The new age will come "out of chaos" from the old. As 33 degrees of the great circle of the earth is 2012 miles, this sign will be at peak alignment at winter solstice, December 21, 2012... exactly when the Mayan calendar ends and their heavenly serpent god returns. This is the "first time" of the Egyptians, when the primordial mound of the earth rose from the starry sea 6,480 ago.

ORIGINAL REVELATION

Students of comparative religions will find interest in the corresponding legends from around the world combining imagery of these heavenly (or elevated) serpents and bearded saviors as well as the beginning of creation and ending of time based on the return of the "one." Many of these gods sailed in a ship portrayed as a serpent moving across the waters of the sky. Jesus was undoubtedly familiar with contemporary analogous themes, and some believe he trumps them when he says to Nathanael, "Hereafter ye shall see heaven open, and the angels of God ascending and descending upon the Son of Man" (Matt. 1.51b). R.V.G. Tasker, Professor of New Testament Exegesis in the University of London, says of this in his lecture "Our Lord's Use of the Old Testament" that Nathanael now learns, "Jesus Himself was the ladder that alone could bridge the gulf between heaven and earth" (13).

Chapter 6

COUNT DOWN
TO 2012

I n May 2005, Cryptoarcheologist David E. Flynn wrote the article, "An Occult Translation of the Roswell Event: Count Down to 2012" for my news service, *RaidersNewsNetwork. com*. This unprecedented feature, a world exclusive, later formed the basis of Flynn's presentation at the 2005 Ancient of Days Conference in Roswell, NM, and since has been quoted by media and print publications around the world, including *Atlantis Rising* and *UFO Magazine* (which published the piece in its entirety in the October/November 2005 issue). Some of the points made by Flynn are so important and fitting at this juncture that Chapter 6 will be dedicated to an excerpt of a significant portion of Flynn's article.

EXCERPT FROM
"AN OCCULT TRANSLATION OF THE
ROSWELL EVENT: COUNT DOWN TO 2012"
BY DAVID E. FLYNN

[Reprinted with slight modification by permission of RaidersNewsNetwork. com and David E. Flynn.]

No UFO conversation goes very long without mention of the Roswell event. It is the pre-eminent story of extraterrestrial folklore. Paradoxically, some say that what occurred near Roswell, NM, in July 1947 will never be entirely known. Others, like our own government, claim it was a simple case of misidentification: no mystery. But there is a mystery, and there is good reason to believe the truth was covered up.

On July 8, 1947, the headlines of *Roswell Daily Record* reported: "RAAF Captures Flying Saucer on Ranch in Roswell Region. The intelligence office of the 509th Bombardment group at Roswell Army Field announced at noon today, that the field has come into possession of a flying saucer." The next day the Roswell headlines featured a retraction by the RAAF: "An examination by the army revealed last night that mysterious objects found on a lonely New Mexico ranch was a harmless high-altitude weather balloon—not a grounded flying disc."

The contrast between these Army statements aroused suspicion immediately. How could Army "intelligence" confuse a balloon with a flying saucer? Witnesses in Roswell had actually observed the disc flying overhead. Their story was featured with the Army's "flying saucer" announcement in the July 8th *Roswell Daily Record*:

Mr. and Mrs. Dan Wilmot...were sitting on their porch at 105 South Penn. last Wednesday night at about ten o'clock when a large glowing object zoomed out of the sky from the southeast, going in a northwesterly direction at a high rate of speed....The object came into view from the southeast and disappeared over the treetops in the general vicinity of six mile hill...It was in sight less then a minute, perhaps 40 or 50 seconds. Wilmot said that it appeared to him to be about 1,500 feet high and going fast. He estimated between 400 and 500 miles per hour....In appearance it looked oval in shape like two inverted saucers, faced mouth to mouth, or like two old type washbowls placed, together in the same fashion....

Balloons do not normally glow or travel 400 miles per hour. Despite the evidence supporting the Army's first announcement, the Roswell incident was effectively removed from public scrutiny for thirty-seven years.

In 1984, James Shandera, a Hollywood movie producer investigating the UFO phenomena, received an anonymously mailed package of 35 mm film. It contained images of a top secret Government report, later named the "Majestic Twelve (or MJ-12) documents." The report had been compiled for review by president Dwight D. Eisenhower. It was marked: "This is a TOP SECRET—EYES ONLY document containing compartmentalized information essential to the national security of the United States."

In the document was a list of twelve American scientists, intelligence officials, and military leaders appointed to assess the remains of an extraterrestrial craft and alien bodies recovered from Roswell, NM, in 1947. One year later, an anonymous tip arrived in the mail addressed to the research associate working with Shandera named Bill Moore. This tip directed Moore to a memo confirming the existence of the MJ-12 documents at the

National Archives. This new information and other evidence that built a case for authenticity of the MJ-12 documents was pieced together by Moore and his associate Stanton Friedman. During the course of their research, Friedman and Moore began to realize that authentication of the MJ-12 documents would be extremely difficult. The investigators even considered the anonymous release of information could be a process of misdirection. Because the origin of the documents was unknown, no one could be sure that they had not originated from a disinformation faction within the government itself. The entire process may have been designed to fail. The release of conflicting or inaccurate information of UFO events by secret factions in government is a well-known hazard of Ufology research. This disinformation technique is used to establish government plausible deniability. But if the release of the MJ-12 documents was not just a convoluted process of disinformation, what other purpose could disclosure of the Roswell event serve?

The Majestic Twelve documents were made public in 1987. Soon the Roswell incident became the most famous UFO incident in history. Roswell raised the possibility that intelligent extraterrestrial life could exist. The anonymous "assistance" given to the investigators of the Roswell event or the manner in which any UFO information is dispensed by our government appears more a program of cultural conditioning than simple fact hiding. If this is true, for what purpose are we being conditioned?

In 1928 the occult visionary Manly P. Hall wrote:

Not only were many of the founders of the United States government Masons, but they received aid from a secret and august body existing in Europe, which helped them to establish this country for A PECULIAR

AND PARTICULAR PURPOSE known only to the initiated few. (*Secret Teachings* XC, XCI)

Hall also wrote:

There exists in the world today, and has existed for thousands of years, a body of enlightened humans united in what might be termed, an Order of the Quest. It is composed of those whose intellectual and spiritual perceptions have revealed to them that civilization has secret destiny...

European mysticism was not dead at the time the United States of America was founded. The hand of the mysteries controlled in the establishment of the new government for the signature of the mysteries may still be seen on the Great Seal of the United States of America. Careful analysis of the seal discloses a mass of occult and Masonic symbols chief among them, the so-called American eagle....The American eagle upon the Great Seal is but a conventionalized phoenix..." (*Secret Destiny*)

"Phoenix," the last word of Hall's statement regarding the founding of America, is key to the "secret destiny" of civilization. It explains the occult design behind the formation of the United States and the events at Roswell. These mysteries can be solved if we understand this one word.

The word "Phoenix" is a derivative of the Greek name for "Phoenicians," ancient people that inhabited the east coast of the Mediterranean Sea. Though called "Phoenicians" (meaning redness) by the Greeks, the Phoenicians referred to themselves as Sidonians. Their capital city was named after Sidon, the first born son of Canaan (son of Ham). Ham was one of the original occupants of Noah's Ark and Noah's youngest son. The Sidonians were considered masters of science and magic. They claimed to possess a civilization existing for 30,000 years. Ancient historians venerated the Sidonians:

- Sidonian navigators were especially sought by the Egyptians, Babylonians, Persians, and Greeks.
- The Greek alphabet was transferred directly from the Phoenician/Sidonian script and applied to the sounds of the language of the Greeks, hence the meaning of the word "phonetic."
- The modern English alphabet is based on the ancient Phoenician/Sidonian script.
- The majority of knowledge ascribed through the ages to the Greeks was given to them first by the Sidonians.
- Pythagoras, considered the ancient father of Free Masonry, was schooled in Sidonia.
- The first phonetic text in existence, the Old Testament, was written in Phoenician characters.
- The first temple of the Hebrews was built in Jerusalem by artisans from Tyre, a city that traded Phoenician capital status with Sidon.

The preeminence of the Phoenician/Sidonian knowledge in ancient civilization is a long guarded occult secret.

But more important than the scientific influence of Sidonia is the fact that the symbolic meaning of Manly Hall's Phoenix represents an age when mankind and extraterrestrials were believed to have lived on earth side by side. Phoenicia was the land of descent of the "Sons of God" described in Genesis 6.

According to the history of every ancient culture in the Middle East, Phoenicia was the first place where beings from heaven came to the earth. The union of these beings with the daughters of Adam produced hybrid offspring, Nephilim (literally in Hebrew, the fallen ones). According to the pseudepigraphic Book of Enoch, the Book of Jubilees, and many other ancient texts, the exact point of descent of the Sons of God was Mt. Hermon in Phoenicia. Through the influence of these heavenly beings and their offspring, men became gifted with knowledge surpassing any that had yet existed. But then came the flood, and symbolically, the Phoenix perished. The heavenly and supernatural bird, keeper of secrets of the past and future, was consumed in the fire of its own making. In other words, the knowledge given to man from heaven was lost in a global cataclysm. According to Genesis 6, the destruction of earth by the flood was in response to the interaction of the Sons of God with the daughters of Adam.

Ancient and modern occult adepts describe the beauty of Phoenix, dazzling and brilliantly colored. It was a perfect symbol for heavenly knowledge manifested on the earth. They believed the power of the Phoenix came from heaven. Its death on earth would only be temporary. The life of the Phoenix could not be extinguished any more than the heavens or knowledge could cease to exist. The Phoenix waited to be born again out of the ashes of its demise.

The symbolic rebirth of the Phoenix did take place in the time after the flood. Nephilim that survived the cataclysm returned to their point of origin in Phoenicia, as recorded in the Old Testament. Canaan, the son of Ham (the cursed son of Noah) once again established civilization amidst the beings that had caused the destruction of the world.

The Nephilim were more powerful and intelligent than

men, but they were earth bound like men. The connection they once had to their heavenly progenitors had been cut. Together with humanity they beckoned the Sons of God to descend as they had before the flood. They built a tower reaching into the heavens. Because of this attempt, it is recorded that the world lost what was left of divine knowledge through its dispersion throughout the earth.

Manly P. Hall refers to this history when writing of the coming world order and the rise of the Phoenix. His understanding of the Phoenix is shared by illumined fraternal orders that have preserved the scattered "sacred" knowledge of the ancients. They anticipate the rise of the Phoenix from the ashes of history. They wait for an age when knowledge will once again descend from heaven. This secret has been hidden in their symbolism and numerology throughout history.

As Benjamin Crème states, "in Freemasonry is embedded the core or the secret heart of the occult mysteries, wrapped up on number, metaphor, and symbol …" (87). According to W. Wynn Westcott: "numbers are a key to the ancient views of cosmogony…spiritually as well as physically…to the evolution of the present human race; all systems of religious mysticism are based upon numerals. The sacredness of numbers…" (15). Finally, "…in Spiritual Numerology, '33' symbolizes the highest spiritual conscious attainable by the human being" (van Buren 161-2).

The numbers 33 and 3 are both featured prominently in occult doctrine. The great significance of the number 33 cannot be fully understood unless it is combined with the most important science of Free Masonry, navigation. The compass and square, the most visible symbols of Masonry are also the basic tools of navigation and map making.

Calculation of speed and location under the heavens is

considered to be the highest form of sacred knowledge from antiquity. Navigation unites time with space and the heavens with the earth. The number 3 is essential to this process. Without the geometry of the 3-sided triangle, establishing location and distance on a map or "triangulation" is impossible. Navigation not only predicts the destination of a traveler on the earth but also the time the traveler will arrive. The most powerful secret held by the occult elite is related to this concept taken to a higher level.

As the navigator can use increments of the earth's latitude and longitude to determine location in space and time, these increments can be measured in the earth itself to reveal the appointed time of humanity's destiny. The following shows why the number 33 and the compass and square are such important symbols of the illumined elite: 33.33 degrees of the great circle of the earth represents 2012 nautical miles. Mount Hermon in Phoenicia, the first location of extraterrestrial influence upon man, lies precisely at 33.33° north and 33.33° east: 2,012 miles from the equator and 2,012 miles from the Paris Meridian, which was often used as the prime meridian throughout history and is the meridian to which many ancient structures are aligned. Additionally, the Knights Templar used the Paris Meridian as the prime meridian. (The Paris Meridian is 2.20 degrees east of the Greenwich Meridian, which was established as the prime meridian at the 1884 International Meridian Conference in Washington DC.) While the latitude measurement is standard, just 33.33 degrees north from the equator to Mt. Hermon, the longitude of the earth based on the Paris Meridian seems to have been regarded as increasingly "sensitive" due to the wider dissemination of knowledge during the industrial revolution and needed to be obfuscated. The 1884 International Meridian Conference in Washington DC was heavily influenced by the eminent Alfred Pike as well as by the elite, other members of Iuminatti, not to mention the Vatican.

To be completely accurate, the number of nautical miles in 33.33 degrees of the earth is actually 2012 .9 (rather than the above stated 2012). This more accurate number of 2012.9 corresponds to the year, month, and day that the ancient Mayans of middle America believed their calendar will end, December 21st, 2012. This is also the year their serpent god and founder of civilization, Quetzalcoatle, will return from heaven.

Does the chosen location of the first connection of heaven with the earth on Mt. Hermon at 33.33° (2012 miles from the equator and the Paris Meridian) set in time the final phase of a new world order in the year 2012? But how is the year 2012 anchored in time? Dates and years were commonly measured from the start of the reign of a king or at the founding of a new city in antiquity. Our modern calendar is aligned to the birth of the Messiah of Israel, Jesus Christ, though even this "anchor point" is not fixed absolutely. There is a debate concerning when exactly Jesus was born. Various researchers have placed the time of Christ's birth at 11 BC, 3 BC, and AD 1. Additionally, our modern calendar was based on earlier versions that were adjusted several times forward or back a number of years by Roman Emperors and Popes. Plus, there has already been a 2012 BC in our calendar, though it was not a remarkable year with respect to knowledge.

Therefore, finding a relationship between AD 2012 and our present age may be the critical way to resolve the uncertainty about how the year 2012 is actually anchored in time. Rather than focusing on the calendar itself, it makes more sense to qualify this future date with references left from the previous encounters of extraterrestrials with humanity. If the sons of God descended to Mt. Hermon with the intention of connecting

33.33 with 2012 navigationally, might they also have placed an additional marker coordinating 2012 with the year of their return?

It appears that they did place such a marker. This is very probably the meaning of the Roswell event; it is a marker (consisting of ancient, sacred numbers) that anchors the year 2012 in our present time. The impact area near Roswell lays 33° north latitude, at a distance 2,012 miles from the equator. When the latitude of the impact site 33° north is multiplied by the universal mathematical constant PI (3.141592657 2)..), the result *wrong!* is 104°, which, coincidentally, is the longitude of the impact site. The value of PI is one of the most important numbers of geometry. Without an understanding of this number, the science of building, architecture, and navigation is not possible. Historians actually base one of the classifications of a true civilization on its achievement of PI.

At Roswell, if PI is multiplied by the latitudes from 33.00 to 33.59, a line with the resultant longitude can be traced showing the precise flight path the disc traveled before impact. This line of coordinates lies southeast to northwest, exactly in the direction the craft appeared to follow according to eye witnesses recorded in the *Roswell Daily Record*, July 8th, 1947: "... (the) large glowing object zoomed out of the sky from the southeast, going in a northwesterly direction at a high rate of speed....The object came into view from the southeast..."

The only place on earth where 33° latitude and 104° longitude exist without lying in an ocean, as these coordinates do south of the equator, or on an uninhabited mountain plateau, as these coordinates do in the eastern hemisphere, is a few miles northwest of Roswell, New Mexico, USA. The sacred number 33 multiplied by PI just happens to produce the location where a flying saucer crashed landed in 1947.

Scientists at the Search for Extraterrestrial Intelligence (SETI) know that a radio message from intelligent life out in space would have to use redundant universal mathematical constants. Universal constants are not dependent on calibration systems but rather on ratios. They function with every counting system that exists. Any signal coming from space that has these numbers stands out against the randomness in the background of space noise. Such a signal would define itself as intelligent and deliberate. Such is the case with the location of the Roswell incident. The odds against a crash location occurring "by chance" precisely at the coordinates that are the product of PI X 33 are astronomical—on the order of millions to one. The location was chosen, therefore, to show a deliberate and intelligent message.

In other words, the Roswell event was not an accident. This is a profound contradiction to its initial appearance. The crash and destruction of the sophisticated flying vehicle with occupants, according to reports, seemed an unplanned disaster. It is exactly because of this appearance that researchers speculated that American radar, used in missile tracking experiments at White Sands testing grounds near Roswell, somehow brought the extraterrestrial vehicle down. However, if the message at Roswell is more than a strange mathematical coincidence, this would also suggest that the crash was staged and the vehicle's occupants sacrificed. By appearing as an accident, the last thing one would look for is a message deposited in the crash location itself.

But there is more to the message than the display of "PI." The Roswell event also incorporates numbers of the earth's dimensions and orientation in space. These numbers interact with each other in patterns similar to those known to exist in occult ritual magic. Though the value of a number may change with placement of the decimal point, the *magical* form of the number remains the same. Numbers that display these characteristics are commonly seen in the practice of "theurgy" or numerology. ("Theurgy describes the practice of rituals, sometimes seen as magical in nature, performed with the intention of invoking the action of God [or other personified supernatural power], especially with the goal of uniting with the divine" [*Wikipedia*].) This patterned interaction of numbers is especially notable in the way the message at Roswell displays the number 19.47 (19.47 has the same magical form as 1947—the year the Roswell event occurred).

To explain further, 19.47° or "19.5" is a universal number signifying the meeting of a tetrahedron with a sphere. The latitude of 19.47° is where three points of the four-sided tetrahedron touch north or south of the equator if the fourth point is anchored at the pole of a rotating sphere. If the number 19.47 were discovered in an extraterrestrial radio signal, SETI scientists would have proof that the broadcasters understood advanced Platonic geometry. As will be later shown, the Roswell message numerologically interconnects 19.47 with the date, latitude, longitude, and distance from the equator of the impact event itself.

Returning to the assertion that the earth's dimensions and orientation in space are incorporated into the Roswell event, the earth is 21,600 nautical miles around. This measurement is based on the ratio of 360 X 60—first used by the Phoenicians and still in use by modern ocean and flight navigators. As far as the earth's orientation in space: the number 6,480 is exactly 1/4th of the total 25,920 years it takes earth to complete one circuit through the signs of the zodiac. This particular number of years—6,480—is unique because it marks the duration between a series of global cataclysms left in earth's historic and geologic record.

Furthermore, in considering the connection of the afore-mentioned numbers with the event at Roswell, **19.**47 (the number suggested by the year of the Roswell crash [1947] and the universal number signifying the meeting of a tetrahedron with a sphere) **appears in relationship with 21,600** (the earth's circumference), **6,480** (1/4th the total of years it takes earth to complete one circuit through the signs of the zodiac and the duration between historic global cataclysms), **and 33.33** (the latitude point of Mt. Hermon and the equivalent of 2012.9 nautical miles from the equator, which raises the possibility of 2012 marking the year of the return of the beings who first descended upon earth via Mt. Hermon). When 21,600 is divided by 33.33 the number 6,480 appears in a variation:

- 21,600/33.3 = 648.06480648064...
- 648.06480648064...divided by 19.47 produces a modification of 33.33:
  648.064806480/19.47 = 33.28
- 33.28° is the exact latitude of the Roswell crash site
- 33.28° multiplied by PI (3.141592653589...) results in a longitude of 104.56°   *correct !*
- 104.56° is the exact longitude of the Roswell crash site

Thus, using the above defined numbers 21,600, 33.33, 6,480, and 19.47 in relationship with each other pinpoints the *exact* coordinates of the disc impact site near Roswell, NM.

Additionally, the number 2012 (the predicted year of the heavenly beings' return) can be calculated with a form of the number of the exact Roswell crash site latitude, 33.28° and a form of the number of the year of the Roswell event itself, 1947:

- 19.47 X 3.328 = 64.80
- Between July 1947 and March 2012 there are 64.80 years.

It is significant that the United States recovered the debris and "alien" bodies of the Roswell crash on the 4th of July 1947. America itself was founded on the same date in 1776. This year was chosen by the occult elite behind the formation of America for a special reason. This reason being: 888 is the sum of the letters in Greek of the name Jesus (each Greek letter represents a number). A second "messiah" (888) plus the first messiah (888) = 1776. America's founding date, 1776, is a number representing a second messiah or the "king" of the World Order. It symbolizes the advent of a god-man on earth.

According to the illuminated elite, as the first messiah came to establish the Kingdom of Heaven, the second illuminated messiah will establish a New World under his rule. Concerning this messiah, Manly P. Hall, wrote: "The outcome of the 'secret destiny' is a World Order ruled by a King with supernatural powers. This King was descended of a divine race; that is, he belonged to the Order of the Illumined for those who come to a state of wisdom then belong to a family of heroes-perfected human beings..." (*The Secret Destiny* 26).

Furthermore, 1776 is related to the latitude and year of the Roswell event. In calculating this connection, one must keep in mind that the average number of days in a year for a century is 364.864 (this is slightly less than 365 because it includes leap years that have an extra day). This figure is produced when the quarter of precession 6,480 is divided by a form of the founding year of America 1776 (the decimal point is moved two spaces to the left).

what?

Wouldn't that make average >365?

- 6,480/17.76 = 364.864648
- 364.864648 X 1776 = 648,000/33.28 (Roswell event latitude) = 19,470

Likewise, the Roswell event longitude is also related to America's birth year 1776:

- 1776/17.076 = 104.0056, (the exact longitude of Roswell crash site is 104.56°)

America has existed from the beginning as an intellectual beacon in the world. It was the first country to achieve super-power status, moving mankind into the space- and nuclear ages. It is the country that continues to shape the political and eco-nomic climate into one that is conducive to a future ruled by a single, heavenly power. And it is the country where the year 2012, as it occurs on our modern calendar, appears to have been (through the Roswell event) supernaturally communicated to humanity as being the date marking the return of the sons of God—a new world order led by an unearthly powered ruler.

❋ ❋ ❋

Following David Flynn's incredible article on Roswell and the year 2012, I sat down with Col. Jesse Marcel Jr., who is admit-tedly the only civilian alive to have handled the UFO "debris" from the Roswell crash site, and he shared information with me, on and off the record. I heard things I had never heard before from ufology's legendary friend. Marcel is almost sev-enty-years-old now and is a soft spoken, gentle man who comes across as ultimately believable. When I asked Jess, as he prefers to be called, if his father—the Intelligence Officer at Roswell Army Air Field at the time of the Roswell event—could have been mistaken about what was recovered during the field investigation, he answered without hesitation, "No way," and then proceeded to tell me why.

When later I pressed about Mogul balloons and Operation Paperclip as alternative theories, he shared at length the number of times he had joined honest investigators in a side-by-side comparison of their "evidence" with his drawings and material examples; each time there was not a single correspondent to what his father had brought home from the ranch that night. Getting to the big questions, I offered, "But of course whatever happened at Roswell, surely it could be explained as top-secret terrestrial technology, right?" As cool as silky water, he looked at me and replied, "Tom, what I saw was not of this earth. Though it was material, I held it in my hands, and the pieces were as light as a feather."

I gave Jess greetings from Stanton Friedman, who together with Bill Moore had brought the Roswell cover-up to international light many years ago, and then I said, "So you, like Stan Friedman, believe the Roswell debris were most likely a physical technology?" Jess smiled and told me how Friedman was such a close family friend. I am not sure he ever did get around to answering my question about technology. However, Col. Marcel, like his father before him, is a career military man (he had just returned from Iraq where as an ear, nose, and throat specialist he was busy patching up soldiers). Over the years he has participated in field investigations of crashed known craft and is very familiar with many hardware components. To this day he has never seen anything resembling the Roswell artifacts.

Marcel then proceeded to tell me an intriguing story about an incident that had happened some years ago, when he was scheduled to be in Washington DC. To this day he does not know how the participants knew where he would be at that particular time. When he arrived at his motel, there was a message waiting for him on the phone in his room. It was from a man we will call Mr. "X." He wanted to meet with Marcel the following day at 1:00 PM in a certain room at the Capital building. Marcel felt uneasy but agreed to go to the meeting. On arrival, he was ushered into the office of Mr. "X," who got right down to business. "X" wanted to talk to Marcel about Roswell, and he asked if Jess would be more comfortable "in a secure room." When Marcel explained that he would not be saying anything he had not said before, "X" pressed the idea of the alternate meeting area, explaining, "Well, maybe I want to tell you something you do not already know."

Leaving the office, they proceeded to the secure room where no listening devices existed, in an area Jess described as "the dungeons of the Capital building." They sat at a table where Marcel noticed a book about alien abductions, UFO technology, and Roswell. "X" tapped on the book with his finger and said outright, "This is not fiction." The mysterious government insider (later identified as Dick D'Amato, an aide to Sen. Robert Byrd) continued talking for a while and then asked Marcel if he knew where the material recovered from the Roswell ranch was being kept. Jess found the question curious and said, "No. Don't you?" "X"'s answer was as enigmatic as the question, so Marcel responded with an inquiry of his own: "If extraterrestrial activity is real, and you guys know it, when is the government planning Official Disclosure of what really happened at Roswell?"

"If it was up to me," "X" said, "we'd be doing it now."

Following a story like that, I just had to ask Col. Marcel if he personally knew of other members of the government and military who also are anticipating a future moment when the representatives of the world's religions and leaders of nations will stand in the well of the United Nations and say, "We have an announcement to make. We are in contact with extraterrestrial intelligence."

Marcel grew silent for a moment, then looked at me and whispered, *"Yes."*

Suddenly the phone rang, and Col. Marcel had to leave the building.

Chapter 7

HUMAN PARTICIPATION
IN TRAVERSING
THE PORTALS

The past several chapters have discussed "them." Whether "they" are labeled as angels and demons, good and bad aliens, gods of mythology, or multidimensional unknowns, history is replete with records of superintelligent beings interacting with the process of human development. While the activity of these beings is frequently overlooked, close collaboration between "them" and architects of society has at times allowed these beings to dictate the course of individuals and/or nations. Ancient iconography actually depicts this collaborative relationship as being between celestials (gods) and terrestrials (humans) and further as being facilitated by stargates, portals, ladders, and other mechanisms through which the separate realities are joined.

This chapter is based on the assumption that the phenomenon of other-dimensionals coming through gates is real and that

humans do play a roll to some extent and under certain circum-
stances in the opening and closing of the portals between the
three-dimensional realm and that of superintelligent beings.

As is referenced in chapter 2, in 1918 famed occultist Aleister
Crowley attempted to create a dimensional vortex that would
bridge the gap between the world of the seen and the unseen.
The ritual was called the Amalantrah Working and according
to Crowley became successful when a presence manifested itself
through the rift. He called the being "Lam" and drew a portrait
of it. The startling image, detailed almost ninety years ago, bears
powerful similarity with "Alien Greys" of later pop culture.

L. Ron Hubbard and Jack Parsons attempted to do this very
thing by inviting the spirit of Babylon through a portal during a
sex ritual. Their hope was to incarnate the whore of Babylon—a
demon child or Gibborim. Parsons wrote that the ritual was
successful (King 161) and that at one point a brownish/yellow
light came through the doorway. At the same moment he said
he was struck by something invisible, and a candle was knocked
out of his hand.

It is interesting that following Crowley's magic portal (which
produced the alien-looking LAM) and Hubbard and Parson's
Babylon Working ritual, Crowley died in 1947—the same year
as the Roswell crash and the same year Kenneth Arnold saw
his flying saucers and sightings of "aliens" increased around the
world. Was a portal indeed opened by these men's invitations?

In more than thirty important biblical passages, the Greek
New Testament refers to an invisible domain or "government"
located in the space between heaven and earth—the kosmos.
According to Ephesians 6.12, this sphere is commanded by
Archons—dominating kosmokrators (rulers of darkness) that
work in and through human political counterparts who, in
turn, command influences of lesser rank until every level of

earthly government can be touched by this power. If we could see through the veil into the dimension of these beings, we would find the atmosphere above and around us alive with good against evil. This is a place where the prize is the souls of men and where legions war for control of its cities and people.

FLYING SERPENT GODS OVER CITIES?

And to the angel of the church in [Pergamum] write; These things saith he which hath the sharp sword with two edges; I know thy works, and where thou dwellest, even where Satan's seat is: and thou holdest fast my name, and has not denied my faith, even in those days wherein Antipas was my faithful martyr, who was slain among you, where Satan dwelleth. (Rev. 2.12-13)

In the letter to the church in Pergamos (Pergamum), verse 13 is enlightening: "I know…where thou dwellest, even where Satan's seat is." The Greek verse reads *Satanos thronos esti*, literally, "Where a throne to Satan is."

At the time of the writing of Revelation, in the Hellenistic kingdoms of Asia Minor—twenty miles from the Aegean Sea and forty miles north of Smyrna—stood the most impressive surviving city built during the conquests of Alexander the Great: Pergamum. Named from the Latin, *pergamentum* (parchment), this was a city known for its great library, massive royal palace, museums, and temples dedicated to the Greek and Roman gods—Zeus, Apollo, Athena, and Asclepius. A theater seating ten thousand people sloped down to the stoa, a column-lined promenade that looked out over the plains below. A leading citizen of ancient Pergamum was Galen, a man gifted in the field of medicine, who was second only to Hippocrates in fame, but not in deed. Galen gathered all the medical knowledge of antiquity into his writings and was considered the supreme authority in medical science for more than a thousand years.

Yet Pergamum, while advanced, was a city under dark influence according to early Christians. The primary problem stood at the base of Pergamum's hill—the shrine of Asclepius, equipped with its own library, theater, sleeping chambers (used in healing rituals), and long underground tunnels joining various other shrines to which people journeyed to receive the healing powers of the serpent god. Aristophanes described how snakes were incorporated into the worship of Asclepius and how they glided between the sleepers at night in the sleeping chambers in Pergamum. On Attic reliefs from the fourth century BC, snakes are depicted licking the patients who slept in the healing chambers of the shrine and cures on display referred to the virtues of this licking.

However, to the newly formed Christian community in Pergamum, Asclepius worship was reminiscent of the serpent in the Garden of Eden, and the snake handling methods used in imploring him were considered an invitation for serpents of "air" to take residence over the city. These convictions were so strong that Christian stone cutters who worked in the quarries around Pergamum refused a commission to fashion a large statue of Asclepius, and for this refusal they were put to death. Some believe that Antipas, who is described in Revelation 2.13 as dying a martyr's death "where Satan dwelleth," was the leader of those slain for resisting Asclepiunism.

Christians in Pergamum were also aware that Apollo, at his famous oracle at Delphi, ordained the worship of Asclepius. The area around Delphi was earlier known by the name Pytho, a chief city of Phocis. In Greek mythology it was Python—the namesake of the city of Pytho—who was the great serpent or demon that dwelt atop the mountains of Parnassus, menacing the area as the chief guardian of the famous oracle at Delphi.

In Acts 16.16 there is another reference to the Python myth. The woman who troubled Paul was possessed with a "spirit of divination." In Greek this means a spirit of Python (a seeress of Delphi, a pythoness) and may reflect what Paul believed—that all such religious practices were demonic, an invitation for serpents of earth, sea, and sky to invade the atmosphere above cities. In Acts 7.41-42 (JB), Stephen refers to the same idea when he says that serving idols is akin to the worship of "the army of heaven."

Therefore, while the city of Pergamum must have been magnificent to the natural eye, evidently there was something over Pergamum that the human eye could not see. As previously mentioned, according to Jesus, Pergamum is *Satanos thronos esti*—a place where Satan's throne is (Rev. 2.12-13), a place dominated by darkness. To have designated Pergamum as a geography under Satan's dominion in this way provides an enlightening diagram of stargate modus operandi.

GOING BEYOND HEBREW BELIEF

In chapter 10 of Daniel, there is another example of specific geography mentioned in league with powerful, invisible forces. According to the Bible, the prophet had been fasting and praying for twenty-one days, hoping the God of Israel would see his fast and grant him revelation of Israel's future, when on the twenty-first day of his fast, the angel Gabriel appears and informs Daniel, "...from the first day thou didst set thine heart to understand, and to chasten thyself before thy God, thy words were heard, and I am come for thy words" (Dan. 10.12).

Yet, if the angel had been dispatched from heaven from the first day, why did it take twenty-one days before he arrived? Gabriel provided the answer by explaining that a powerful

Persian _influence_ had opposed him for twenty-one days. Not until Michael, the archangel, came to assist in this conflict was Gabriel free to continue his journey (Dan. 10.13).

In Persian theology, this opposing spirit would have been identified as Ahriman—enemy of Ahura Mazda. According to Persian religion, Ahriman was the Death-dealer—the powerful and self-existing evil spirit, from whom war and all other evils had their origin. He was the chief of the cacodaemons, or fallen angels, expelled from heaven for their sins. After their expulsion, the cacodaemons took up their abode in the space between heaven and earth and there established their domain called _Ahriman-abad._ From the sky above, the cacodaemons could intrude upon and attempt to corrupt humans below.

In Daniel, this same negative influence is described as the prince of the kingdom of Persia, which is now Iraq/Iran (Dan. 10.20). Later, Gabriel informed Daniel that upon his departure the "prince of Grecia shall come" (Dan. 10.20), thus giving additional indication of geographies ruled over—or at least greatly influenced by—atmospheric forces.

HEBREW DEVILS OR INTERGALACTIC TRAVELERS?

That something involving superintelligence has visited earth from the beginning of time, interacted with humans, and behaved in ways that is defined as both good and evil is believed by the vast majority of persons. It would also seem to be supported by physical and historical phenomena. Consider the following:

- Around the world, continents are dotted by thousands of prehistoric and colossal pictographs that presumably could not have been designed from the surface of the earth.

- Centuries before the colossus of Rome, civilizations around the world built pyramids out of stones so large and with such astronomical precision that the same engineering feats could not be repeated until very recently, and with large machines.

- Fourteen hundred years before Christ, the Assyrians depicted Saturn with rings and chronicled the detailed movements of the moon. European astronomers did not make the same deductions until the seventeenth century AD.

- Over six thousand years ago, Sumerians recorded knowledge of the solar system on cylinder seals with the sun at the center of the universe and eleven bodies surrounding it, including Pluto (which we only recently discovered) and a tenth planet called Nibiru. With the moon and the sun included, it is the twelfth planet, thus some see this as the origin of the twelve gods, twelve tribes, twelve titans etc.

- The Antikethyra mechanism is the world's oldest analogue computer, dated to about 150-100 BC. It was found in the Antikythera wreck off the Greek island of Antikythera, between Kythera and Crete. The computer contains at least thirty inter-locking gear-wheels and precisely measures astronomical movements including lunar and solar eclipses and planetary positions.

These and hundreds of other unexplained discoveries have caused some to wonder where ancient civilizations came to understand advanced astronomy and technology. Some contend that extraterrestrial intelligence traveled from distant planets (or other dimensions), imparted galactic wisdom to people around the globe, and then departed through a wormhole or "stargate," leaving behind promises of returning someday. Students of theology have picked up on this concept in recent years, blending it with traditional demonology and suggesting that demons were (and are) mimicking visitors from another world in order to deceive the human race.

THE WORDS OF PAUL AGAIN

"And then shall that Wicked [one] be revealed…whose coming is after the working of Satan with all power and signs and lying wonders" (2 Thess. 2.8-9). The "lying wonders" of 2 Thessalonians are, according to one theory, end-time flying saucers that will be piloted by creatures who appear to be advanced humanoids but who are in fact evil spirits on a quest to conquer and destroy the creation of God.

Surprisingly, secular Ufologists are partially to blame for advancing the "evil flying geniuses" theory. In some cases they too postulate interaction between humans and ET as malevolent. Whitley Strieber, author of *Communion* and other books on the subject of UFOs, and reportedly a victim of "Alien abduction," once wrote:

> There are worse things than death, I suspected. And I was beginning to get the distinct impression that one of them had taken an interest in me. So far the word demon had never been spoken among the scientists and doctors who were working with me. And why should it have been? We were beyond such things. We were a group of atheists and agnostics, far too sophisticated to be concerned with such archaic ideas as demons and angels. (126)

Professor Elizabeth L. Hillstrom in her book *Testing the Spirits* says that a growing number of academics have concluded that UFOnauts are synonymous with historical demonism:

> Vallée 's explanation of UFOs is the most striking because of its parallels with demonic activity. UFO investigators have noticed these similarities. Vallée himself, drawing from extra biblical literature on demonic activities, establishes a number of parallels between UFOnauts and demons....Pierre Guerin, a UFO researcher and a scientist associated with the French National Council for Scientific Research, is not so cautious: "The modern UFOnauts and the demons of past days are probably identical." Veteran researcher John Keel, who wrote *UFOs: Operation Trojan Horse* and other books on the subject, comes to the same conclusion: "The UFO manifestations seem to be, by and large, merely minor variations of the age-old demonological phenomenon." (207-208)

Although Ufologists of various creeds may disagree on the meaning of a particular ET phenomenon, many assert language that defines UFOs and extraterrestrial intelligence in angeological and demonological terms, including rhetoric about the gods of mythology and stargates. The following is a short list of the "demonological" beings described by moderns and ancients as having come through these portals:

Abaddon—Hebrew, "the destroyer"

Adramelech—Samarian devil, chancellor of the infernal regions

Agathodemon—Egyptian serpent devil with a human head

Ahpuch—Mayan devil

Arimanius—Persian devil, chief of the cacodaemons (fallen angels)

Alastor—chief executioner to the monarch of Hades, a cruel demon

Aldinach—Egyptian devil

Amon—Egyptian ram-headed devil

Apollyon—Greek synonym for Satan

Asmodeus—Hebrew demon of sensuality and luxury

Astaroth—Phoenician goddess of lasciviousness

Arioch—demon of vengeance

Baalberith—Canaanite devil

Balaam—Hebrew devil of greed

Baphomet—goat-headed symbol and name for Satan

Bast—Egyptian devil of pleasure

Beelzeboul—"lord of the height," Satan as the prince of the air

Beelzebub—Satan, prince of devils, lord of those that fly

Behemoth—Hebrew personification of Satan as an elephant

Beherit—Syriac name for Satan

Bile'—Celtic god of hell

Bisclaveret—British demon, werewolf

Bogey—Slavonic demon, bug-a-boo, the bogeyman

Boh—Welsh spirit or magic word used to frighten children ("boo")

Chemosh—Moabite demon

Cimeries—African devil-riding black horse

Coyote—American Indian devil

Dagon—Philistine avenging devil of the sea

Damballa—voodoo serpent god

Demogorgon—forbidden Greek name of the devil

Diabolus—Greek fallen one

Diablo—Spanish devil

Emma-O—Japanese ruler of Hell

Euronymous—Greek prince of death

Fenriz—son of Loki, a wolf devil

Gorgo—dim. of Demogorgon

Haborym—Hebrew synonym for Satan

Hanon-Tramp—French demon who suffocates children at
  night

Hecate—Greek devil of the sea and witchcraft later joined
  to Diana

Incubus—male demon of seduction, child of nightmares

Kali—daughter of Shiva and high priestess of the Thuggees

Kelpie—Scottish demon

Kernos—Celtic oak-god of the underworld, worshiped by
  druids

Lilith—Hebrew female devil who presides over the succubae

Loki—Teutonic devil of mischief

Mammon—Aramaic god of wealth and power

Mandragoras—demon who possesses idols, fetishes, and
  voodoo dolls

Mania—Etruscan goddess of hell

Mantus—Etruscan god of hell

Marduk—god of the city of Babylon

Mastema—Hebrew synonym for Satan

Melek Taus—Yezidi devil

Mephistopheles—Greek devil who shuns light

Metztli—Aztec goddess of the night

Mictian—Aztec god of death

Midgard—son of Loki, serpent devil

Milcom—Ammonite devil

Moloch—Phoenician and Canaanite devil

Mormo—Greek king of ghouls

Naamah—Hebrew female devil of seduction
Nergal—Babylonian god of Hades
Nihasa—Arnerican Indian devil
Nija—Polish god of the underworld
0-Yama—Japanese name of Satan
Paigoel—Hindu demon
Pan—Greek god of lust, later relegated to devildom
Pluto—Greek god of the underworld
Proserpine—Greek queen of the underworld, confused
with Hecate
Pwcca—Welsh name for Satan
Rahu—Hindu devil, "the tormenter"
Rakshasa—Indian demon
Red-Man—French demon of the tempests
Rimmon—Syrian devil
Sabazious—Phrygian devil
Saitan—Enochian equivalent of Satan
Samana—Aryan god, the "Grim Reaper"
Sammael—Hebrew devil, "venom of god"
Samnu—Asian demon
Sedit—American Indian devil
Seik Kasso—Burmese demon who possesses trees
Seiktha—Burmese demon
Sekhmet—Egyptian goddess of vengeance
Set—Egyptian devil
Shaitan—Arabic name for Satan
Shiva—Hindu demon of destruction
Spunkie—Scottish demon
Succubus—female demon of seduction, child of nightmares
Supay—Inca god of the underworld
Swawm—Burmese demon, vampire
T'an-mo—Chinese counterpart of Satan

Tchort—Russian name for Satan
Tezcatlipoca—Aztec god of hell
Thamuz—Sumerian god, later relegated to devildom
Thoth—Egyptian devil of magic
Tunrida—Scandinavian female devil
Typhon—Greek personification of Satan
Yaotzin—Aztec god of hell
Yen-Lo-Wang—Chinese ruler of hell

Chapter 8

FACT AND FICTION: QUETZALCOATL'S RETURN

The movie version of the popular game "Doom" staring Dwayne "The Rock" Johnson opens with narration describing an incredible discovery—an ancient teleportation device called "Ark"—which links the planet Earth with Mars. An archeological team goes through the stargate and begins research at the Olduvai station on Mars. While investigating humanoid remains uncovered on the red planet, they unwittingly open a door, and all hell breaks loose. A legion of nightmarish creatures of unknown origin comes through the portal to destroy them.

If this all sounds like the plot to our current book— *Nephilim Stargates: The Year 2012 and the Return of the Watchers*—it is because the makers of "Doom" borrowed from the same mythologies we've been discussing concerning dimensional portals or "doorways" through which beings of good and evil pass.

In our latest book *The Ahriman Gate* (which is filled with these types of cryptic metaphors and understood by adepts of ufology), my wife Nita and I fictionalized that the planet Mars is indeed a prison where entities who rebelled against the Creator God during a past distant war are sealed. When the Ahriman "stargate" is opened, the enclosures slide apart, releasing among other things, Quetzalcoatl, the Feathered-Serpent deity of ancient Mesoamerica. Nita and I selected this myth during plot development due to the significance of associated history and prophecy related to these myths. The great cycle of the Mayan calendar's Long Count and a 26,000 year planetary cycle in the Aztec calendar end on December 21, 2012. How interesting it is that of all possible dates, modern scientists now say we will reach Solar Maximum in 2012, which will vastly increase sunspots, affect airline flights, global positioning satellites, and electrical transmissions. According to the Maya, it will also be a time when the sky opens and Quetzalcoatl returns. According to *The Ahriman Gate*, this will not be a positive thing. We read:

> Three hours later OGS Maintenance Director Kevin Thompson stumbled from the MISS air lock and fell flat on his face in the Martian terrain. He was drunk as a skunk and evidently thought it was funny. At least he'd remembered to put on his Extravehicular Mobility Unit (EMU) spacesuit before venturing outside the Inhabitable Structure.
>
> Managing to get back on his feet, he began singing a song by Don McLean.
>
> > *Did you write the book of love...and do you believe*
> > *in God above...'cause the Bible tells you so?...And*
> > *do you believe in Rock and Roll...can music save*

your mortal soul...and can you teach me how to dance real slow?...

Inside the MISS, the sound engineer who was watching Kevin turned his helmet-cam and microphone off. Kevin's singing was awful, and the cam's recording of the prehistoric Avenue of the Dead passing erratically beneath his feet was as boring as it could get. Kevin had taken his turn at perimeter check a thousand times before and hadn't needed any help. He could do it this time without being monitored, even if he was as drunk as everybody else planned on getting.

Jack be nimble, Jack be quick, Jack Flash sat on a candle stick, 'cause fire is the devil's only friend.... And as I watched him on the stage...my hands were clenched in fists of rage...no angel born in hell could break that Satan's spell...

❈ ❈ ❈

Moving silently near the south side of the Great Mars Pyramid, the ground responded to the *human* insertion of the Nibiruan Key by gliding open and spewing acrid smoke into the Martian atmosphere. Quetzalcoatl, that hoary dragon that had relished the sacrifice of tens of thousands of ancient earthlings, peered menacingly up from the abyss. It had been imprisoned there during the Great War with Michael, the chief prince of Israel. Now it detected an approaching heartbeat and smiled demonically, warmed by the notion that business was about to resume. Heartbeats were such a delightful thing, especially when ripped from the chest and offered in sacrifice to the Feathered Serpent.

Quetzalcoatl heard singing:

> *And as the flames climbed high into the night...to light the sacrificial rite...I saw Satan laughing with delight...the day the music died...*

Spontaneously he raced from his prison, his vast serpentine belly slithering along the ancient stone-way so meticulously aligned with the Dog Star Sirius, honing in on the vulnerable lush.

❀ ❀ ❀

Kevin thought he saw something moving in the middle of the ancient city, near the Well of Sacrifice. Was it a set of eyes? Crouching, sliding along the ground? Nah, couldn't be. Too big! Plus nothing could survive outside an EMU anyway.

> *And in the streets the children screamed...the lovers cried and the poets dreamed...but not a word was spoken...the church bells all were broken...And the three men I admire most...the Father, Son, and Holy Ghost...they caught the last train for the coast...the day the music died...*

❀ ❀ ❀

Quetzalcoatl waited until Kevin floundered inside the City Center, to the area near the prehistoric flat-topped Pyramid and the gigantic Chacmool altar where human abductees were brought by the Grays and sacrificed to the god. He waited and remembered the sweet taste of blood, thick and satisfying like summer honey upon his forked tongue.

> *Bye, Bye, Miss American Pie....Drove my Chevy to the levee, but the levee was dry....Them good ole boys were drinking whiskey and rye...singing this'll be the day that I die....This'll be the day that I die...*

Quetzalcoatl circled Kevin, closing to within several yards before charging him. The demon raised its ten-foot-wide head and leered into the inebriated eyes. Kevin teetered as if trying to decide what he was looking at, but was too late. In a flash Quetzalcoatl clamped his razor-like incisors around his right arm, biting through the tender meat and cutting off the appendage at the shoulder, knocking him to the ground. Kevin reacted as if he was so drunk he didn't realize what had happened.

"H-hey! Whad's goin' on?" he slurred, trying to set up and attempting to use both arms. He flailed sideways as the poisonous atmosphere began seeping in around the missing arm's stub, taking his breath away.

Quetzalcoatl leaned forward and smiled, allowing Kevin to focus on the arm piece dangling from his mouth.

Kevin looked confused, then burst into screaming as he began kicking at the demon, bouncing rocks and dust off the monster's scaly hide.

Trembling with delight, Quetzalcoatl laughed and chewed the mouthful of arm, grinding it in his teeth. His nocturnal eyes, dead and predatory, rolled up like a great white shark's as he lurched forward and slurped the rest of Kevin's body into his hyperextended jaws.

Turning violently, he dragged Kevin down the Avenue of the Dead, over the rough pathway toward the Chacmool, shredding his waist with his fangs as he went, deep enough to torture but not enough to kill him. Seconds later, near the ancient altar, he thrust his forked tongue into Kevin's chest cavity and scooped out his heart, slapping it on the Chacmool with a crimson splash. Flipping the remainder of Kevin's carcass into his hideously large gullet, he ground the human remains into oblivion.

※ ※ ※

An hour later, at Area 51's Mission Control, a male voice crackled over the radio. "Omega Control, Omega Control. This is Outpost Alpha, do you copy?"

"This is Omega Control, Alpha, we copy."

"Omega, this is a level-ten message. Repeat, a level ten, coded high priority."

"Acknowledged, Alpha. You are clear to proceed with level-ten transmission."

"Omega, we've got unknowns. Kevin Thompson is gone and we have mass tango movement near the city center."

"*Tango*, Alpha?"

"Mass tango movement. Betty Lou indicates one hundred sixty-four thousand dots and climbing," the man said, meaning the MISS computer was picking up unknown life forms on the Martian terrain.

"Have you checked Betty Lou, is she operating correctly?"

"She is…and we have visual verification from the Great Pyramid cameras."

"You're sure the dots read organic…not mechanical or electrical?"

"Yes, sir. Looks like lava flowing out of the ground near the pyramid's edge. Flowing up and breaking into organic strands. Cameras twenty-three through twenty-eight near the Face are also picking up ground movement, but no dots there yet."

And what about Kevin? You said he's gone?"

"Nobody knows what happened to him, He simply disappeared. He was conducting a perimeter check when his tag went straight line. We're still looking for his signal…thought we had a heartbeat earlier… could've been…eh…wait a minute.…Betty Lou says we're at three hundred sixty-seven thousand dots at the pyramid now. Gains seem to be doubling every few seconds."

"Do the signatures indicate random or intelligent movement?"

"I would say intelligent. Dots…eem to be oving toward the Face, the Cit…nter, and…oming…ward the MISS."

"Say again, Alpha, you're breaking up. Did you say the dots are moving toward the MISS?"

Static.

"Alpha, this is Omega Control, do you copy, over?"

Static.

"Alpha, do you read, this is Omega Control."

"WHAT THE H...IS THA..."

"Alpha, say again."

"OMEGA ONTROL, THEY'RE BREAKING INTO TH...OMEGA, WE'RE UNDER ATTACK! THE...AKES, GIANT SNAKES!"

"Alpha, this is Omega Control. What is your situation?"

At once the microphone cracked and Omega Control heard what sounded like crunching, hissing, then gurgling and automatic weapons fire, a Russian briefly yelling profanities, and suddenly abrupt silence.

"Alpha, this is Omega Control, do you copy?... Alpha, do you copy?...Alpha, this is Omega Control, report please...Alpha?"

❀ ❀ ❀

Katherine was dreaming again, and for the first time her vision was different. As she hung from the cliff's edge, looking out over the sea, the millions of apelike monstrosities swimming in the waters below her rose up and stood in uniform columns like soldiers preparing to march.

The great dragon came out of the waters too, metamorphosing into a strange yet desirable man wearing a ten-horned crown. He walked upon the water and sat down upon a coal black throne, facing the giant army. Speaking with the dragon's voice, he said:

"Come forth flying serpents, you deceptive ones with your Gray legions. Come forth, for the time of my wrath is come. The humans have chosen the forbidden technology, and a body has been prepared me. I will be born the perditious son of their choosing. At their invitation I will walk the earth and enslave the Most High's creation. I will reclaim my former glory, the glory I had when I governed the Galaxy, before the time of the Fall. I will revisit the stones of fire, Mars and Nibiru, and I will conquer those who wear my mark when I am called the Beast."

Suddenly the sea divided and rolled back, revealing a subterranean world filled with fiery-eyed serpents crawling atop each other inside a hidden chaos. Katherine watched as the reptiles transmogrified into well-dressed men in black suits. The MIB crawled from the pit and took command positions in front of the giant army. Dark glasses covered their elliptical eyes, but couldn't hide what Katherine knew—the men in black were reptilian demons. Reptilian demons were men in black. What did that mean?

She awoke, and screamed. A man in a black suit stood over her.

"Now you and the other cow ssshall come with me," Apol Leon slurred with a demented grin. [Read more about *The Ahriman Gate* at http://www.AhrimanGate.com.]

❋ ❋ ❋

Fiction, right? Yes, but…

In 1997, popular radio host Art Bell on his program *Coast*

to Coast asked eminent theologian and former Jesuit priest, Malachi Martin why the Vatican was heavily invested in the study of deep space at Mt. Graham Observatory in southeastern Arizona. As a retired professor of the Pontifical Biblical Institute, Father Martin was uniquely qualified to hold in secret information pertaining to the Vatican's Advanced Technology Telescope (VATT) project at the Mount Graham International Observatory (MGIO). Martin's answer ignited a firestorm of interest among Christian and secular Ufologists:

> **Father Martin:** Because the mentality, the attitude, mentality amongst those who [are] at the higher levels, highest levels of Vatican administration and geopolitics, know that, now, knowledge of what's going on in space, and what's approaching us, could be of great import in the next five years, ten years. (Martin)

The cryptic words *"...what's approaching us, could be of great import in the next five years, ten years,"* was followed in subsequent interviews with discussion of a mysterious "sign in the sky" that Father Martin believed was approaching from the North. Martin passed away in 1999, but not before allegedly telling his good friend Art Bell "a secret," which some believe related to the space "object" and the five-to-ten-year timeframe.

We stand today at the threshold of Father Martin's words. Yet Martin's historic dialogue is seen as a "sign" by many Ufologists. If ET reality is confirmed, most believe, the Vatican will play an important role during Official Disclosure. Learned researchers therefore keep an open ear for hints by the Vatican that disclosure is nearing.

Martin is not the only priest to have believed something is approaching. Argentinian Jesuit priest and astrophysicist, José

Funes told an international conference in Rome a couple years ago that "extraterrestrials exist and are our brothers" ?! (Cosmiverse). In April 2000, Zecharia Sitchin sat down with leading Vatican theologian, Monsignor Corrado Balducci and discovered that the idea of ancient astronauts creating man is "...something that Christianity is coming around to..." (Sitchin).

deception! *aargh!*

Ruth Gledhill reported not long ago:

There is probably intelligent life elsewhere in the Universe, and there is evidence in the Bible to suggest that it could be Christian, according to the Roman Catholic Church.

In a document published by the Catholic Truth Society, the official publisher for the Vatican, a papal astronomer speculates that "sooner or later, the human race will discover that there are other intelligent creatures out there in the Universe."

Brother Guy Consolmagno, a Jesuit, who is one of the Vatican's leading astronomers, concedes that he could be wrong. Ultimately, he says, "We don't know." But in the new book, part of the *Explanations* series designed to explain Catholic teaching in everyday language, he says that part of his hunch is scientific. With so many billions of planets, stars and galaxies, he says, "surely, somewhere in that number, there must be other civilised, rational beings."

To back up his hunch that the aliens will have been subject to Christ's saving grace, he cites the verses from John's Gospel known as the Good Shepherd passage. In John 10.14-16, Jesus says: "I am the Good Shepherd.... I have other sheep that do not belong to this fold. I must bring them also, and they will listen to My voice. So there will be one flock, one Shepherd."

Only one week before the article above, a very mysterious sign in the sky was captured on film by security cameras in the Mexican town of Branches Arizpe, Coahuila. The unusual object expanded, contracted, and pulsated. The operator of Public Security, Brown Elsa, declared:

> We approximately received a call to the 2:50 a.m., was a commander, to say us that we showed ourselves to the window to see a very luminous star of colors and as to the 5 minutes we received another call and we came to observe by the window, was an object greater than a star…when noticing that it changed of colors we decided to focus it with the urban camera and we realized that was taking circular form, until we saw that it was a strange object. (Cid)

What caught our attention at *RaidersNewsNetwork.com* was commentary by investigator Jaime Maussan, who described the unusual object as a "UFO from a cosmic short cut or dimensional doorway" (Cid).

Of course when thinking of the history of the Catholic Church, appearing saviors, extraterrestrial intelligence, flying discs, and signs in the sky, one cannot help but remember the story that took place in Fatima, Portugal, in 1917, between three children named Lucia, Francisco, and Jacinta and a brilliant apparition they thought to be the Virgin Mary. Lucia described her as a little lady "more brilliant than the sun, and she radiated a sparkling light from her person, clearer and more intense than that of a crystal filled with glittering water and transpierced by the rays of the most burning sun" (Thompson). Because some people doubted the claims, the girls asked the apparition to provide a "sign" for the masses. On October 13, 1917, 70,000 people including what the Catholic Church after thirteen years of investigation called "persons of all categories and of all social classes, believers and non-believers, journalists of the principal Portuguese newspapers" (Thompson) and the educated elite gathered in the pouring rain in a field in Fatima to witness the promised miracle. Then, shortly after noon, the storm clouds abruptly rolled back and a strange fragrance filled the air. What at first looked like the sun appeared as a flat silver disc revolving on its own axis. The object plunged toward the crowd, zigzag-ing erratically across the sky, causing thousands of the witnesses—some who had come to mock the claims as superstitious exaggerations—to fall to their faces in repentance. The Reverend General Vicar of Leiria, one of the witnesses, thought it was the Virgin Mary in an "aeroplane of light," an "immense globe, flying westwards, at moderate speed. It irradiated a very bright light" (Thompson). Another witness, Dr. Almeida Garrett, a professor of Coimbra, described it this way:

> The sun had broken through the thick layer of clouds. It seemed to be drawing all eyes and I saw it as a disc with a clean cut rim, luminous and shining, but which did not hurt the eyes. The clouds did not obscure the light of the sun; one could fix one's eyes on this brazier of heat and light without pain in the eyes or blinding of the retina. The sun's disc spun around on itself in a mad whirl—then, whirling wildly, seemed to loosen itself from the firmament and advance threateningly upon the earth as if to crush us with its huge fiery weight. (Thompson)

Many other witnesses at Fatima described the fiery disc that appeared through an opening in the sky, descended in a rush, moved erratically overhead, and then flew away. Is this, or something like it, what Father Martin was looking for? A dimensional doorway, a Stargate, through which *something or somebody* would arrive in the last days? We have reasons to believe this *could* be the case and that the "what" that is "approaching" earth has been under study for some time. In *The Ahriman Gate*, we refer to the "what" that is coming and have reasons to believe a deadline for disclosure related to the event is upon us.

Time is running out...and whether we like it or not...*something* is headed Earth's way.

Chapter 9

TAKING HUMAN FORM
AND ALIEN ABDUCTIONS

"...unto them were committed the oracles of God" (Rom. 3.1-2).

When the apostle Paul wrote to the church at Rome concerning the oracles (*logion*, "divine utterances"), which God gave to the Hebrews, he was referring to the revelations of the Old Testament Law and Prophets. In the Bible, the word "oracle" means "supernatural utterance." It can also refer to devices used in the production of divine utterances. Thus the Bible *is* an oracle, as was the Urim and Thummim (sacred devices) of the Old Testament. When men or women speak as true prophets of God, they likewise are considered oracles "of God" (1 Pet. 4.11).

Synchronous to Paul's time, pagans held similar beliefs concerning their sacred texts and devices. Ancient Oracles of Egypt, Greece, and Rome were the most famous in antiquity and provided a portal to the invisible world of gods through Oracles at Delphos, Delos, Ammon, Dodona, The Roman Augurs, The Sibylline Books, and others.

Oracles of one form or another have existed throughout

time and around the world for one simple reason: they ostensibly prove the existence of other-dimensional intelligence and provide methods for conversing with and/or inviting through mystical doorways the voices, messages, and presence of other-dimensional beings. While people of all faiths have embraced oracular phenomena (including those outside Jewish/Christian circles), the Bible, Talmud, and associated texts have been widely received as divinely oracular by various religious sects where verses can be interpreted as supporting desired ideas of "God," reincarnation, spirit communing, extraterrestrials, and the afterlife.

Yet, in the quest for other-dimensional contact, some non-Judeo/Christians reach beyond the "confines" of the Bible into the veiled world of esoteric rituals, utterances, visualization, channeling, and other methodology.

On this subject, I once gave a lecture about oracles and the "death of the Olympian gods." I boldly proclaimed that Christianity had swept the globe and that, as far as I knew, not a living person remained on earth that bowed in reverence to Apollo or consulted at his sacred shrines. The speech was received with rousing applause by the audience, and I sold some tapes. The only problem was I was wrong. Apollo's Oracle at Delphi, the most famous oracle of antiquity, is in ruins. But the worship of the Olympian god, and the order of his Pythian priestesses, are actively involved in modern paganism. The fact is it is unclear if the worship of Apollo or the consulting of his oracles ever ceased. There is some evidence that generational witches may have continued the worship of Apollo and the secrets of Pythian divination for centuries. Whether or not that is true, the admirers of Apollo number in the tens of thousands today. This is primarily because Apollo is an oracle god, and his seekers gain "divine audience." Unlike other underworld spirits, Apollo audibly communicates (at times with amazing accuracy in antiquity) through the vocal chords of the pythoness to his followers. This characteristic originally caused, and apparently continues to cause, tremendous cult popularity for Apollo.

The Greek historian, Herodotus (considered the Father of History), recorded an interesting Apollonian event. Croesus, the king of Lydia, expressed doubt regarding the accuracy of Apollo's Oracle at Delphi. To test the oracle, Croesus sent messengers to inquire of the Pythian prophetess as to what he, the king, was doing on a certain day. The priestess surprised the king's messengers by visualizing the question, and formulating the answer, before they arrived. A portion of the historian's account says:

…the moment that the Lydians (the messengers of Croesus) entered the sanctuary, and before they put their questions, the Pythoness thus answered them in hexameter verse: "… *Lo! on my sense there striketh the smell of a shell covered tortoise, Boiling now on a fire, with the flesh of a lamb, in a cauldron. Brass is the vessel below, and brass the cover above it.*" These words the Lydians wrote down at the mouth of the Pythoness as she prophesied, and then set off on their return to Sardis… [when] Croesus undid the rolls . . . [he] instantly made an act of adoration…declaring that the Delphic was the only really oracular shrine.…For on the departure of his messengers he had set himself to think what was most impossible for any one to conceive of his doing, and then, waiting till the day agreed on came, he acted as he had determined. He took a tortoise and a lamb, and cutting them in pieces with his own hands, boiled them together in a brazen cauldron, covered over with a lid which was also of brass. (Herodotus, book 1, verse 47)

The *deity* Apollo established substantial reverence through such interaction and apparently continues to do so. On the Internet there are numerous Web sites today dedicated to the modern worship of Apollo, where the methods and sacred locations of current Pythian oracular activity are taught.

Besides Pythian, ancient oracles revived by participants of various movements currently include interpreting the flame of candles, the organs of animals, the behavior of water, and the whispering of wind through the leaves of trees.

Tree oracles, such as the necromantic oak tree of Zeus at Dodona, were among the most popular oracles of the ancient world. This was due in part to the belief that the root of the tree extended into the lower world, and thus the tree was connected to the underworld dead. Some claim 2 Samuel 5.24 is a scriptural account of King David consulting with tree oracles, and they point out that Jehovah instructed David to "smite the host of the Philistines" after he heard "the sound of a going in the tops of the mulberry trees"(2 Sam. 5.24).

Yet, another and more important reason why animate objects such as trees, animals, and similar organic structures are important aspects of oracle-portals is that "vital energy" associated with three-dimensional life forms may be required as construct material for achieving incarnation by other-dimensional beings.

In *The Invisible College: What a Group of Scientists Has Discovered about UFO Influences on the Human Race*, Jacques Vallée writes:

In order to materialize and take definite form, these entities seem to require a source of energy; a fire or a living thing—plant, a tree, a human medium (or contactee). Our sciences have not reached a point where they can offer us any kind of working hypothesis for this process. But we can speculate that these beings need living energy which they can reconstruct into physical form. Perhaps that is why dogs and animals tend to vanish in flap areas. Perhaps the living cells of those animals are somehow used by the ultraterrestrials to create forms which we can see and sense with our limited [three-dimensional] perceptions. (Vallée 233)

One of the early influences in my life, Dr. Kurt E. Koch, writes similarly in his book *Christian Counseling and Occultism* on teleplastic morphogenesis occurring in six degrees:

The first stage is the emission and separation of veil-like, gauze-like, slimy substances of rubbery elasticity from the body cavities of the medium….The second stage is the formation of body parts such as outline, arms, legs, head, etc.…The third stage is the solidification into complete shadowy forms, which appear as phantoms near the medium….In these three stages we have purely visual materialization phenomena. In the next three stages we move on to active and passive manifestations of energy by the phenomenon.

The fourth stage shows a combination of materialization phenomena with telekineses. The medium is in a position to display energy at a distance by means of an *unknown remote power* [emphasis added]….The fifth stage of the materialization is the penetration of matter….The sixth stage of materialization…is…metamorphosis into animal shapes. (Koch 165-167)

As far back as 1629, in the *Tractatus Theologicus*, Adam Tanner interpreted the same activity as the morphogenesis of demons:

> They often form for themselves bodies from impure air or vapors and exaltations or clouds mixed with air. To the air water is added, earth, mud, sulphur, resin, wood. Sometimes too there are added bones from the corpses of animals or condemned men, at times too from the semen of beasts and men and such like manner. (*Tractatus Theologicus* 62)

"ANGELIC BEINGS" USING CREATED MATTER TO EMBODY THEMSELVES?

As if on queue, angels (perceived as both fallen and unfallen) have become one of the most popular oracular-entities of modern spiritualists. Dozens of New Age books over the last decade describe methods of communicating with and/or manifesting spirits through the "assistance" of angels. Some such titles are self explanatory, such as: *Ask Your Angels: A Practical Guide to Working with the Messengers of Heaven to Empower and Enrich Your Life* and *Angels Within Us: A Spiritual Guide to the Twenty-two Angels that Govern Our Lives*.

In one publication we discover the interesting identity of one of these beings as the author describes his encounter with his angel-oracle:

> The Swirling fog began to dissipate, and I could see the flicker of a light ahead—a darting, pulsating glow resembling a fire-fly. I paused for a moment to observe, and

the tiny flare expanded in size and appeared as a small full moon touching the earth. As I moved closer to the radiance, it suddenly changed into a vertical beam, a pillar of transparent light.

"Are you the angel I am seeking?" I asked.

The soft yet powerful feminine voice replied, "I am the Angel of Creative Wisdom."

"Do you have a name?"

"Some have called me Isis [emphasis added] ," she said, and with those words the pillar of light slowly materialized to reveal the face and form of a beautiful woman wearing a flowing white robe trimmed in gold. (Price 2-3)

It appears that at least some of the beings that came through ancient stargates and dimensional portals continue to do so. In this case, "Isis" is identified as a New Age "angel."

While such angel-oracles are undoubtedly popular among New Age devotees, the most curious form of oracular activity recently reinvigorated is the *Psychomanteum*, a simple, yet eerie method for opening dimensional portals. A chair, placed in front of a large mirror in a dark room, serves as the oracle. Once positioned on the chair, the occupant stares into the mirror and waits for contact with ET or the ghosts of the dearly departed. In ancient times, the Psychomanteum's mirror-system for communicating with "spirits" was employed by primitive Greeks in gloomy underground caverns called "halls of visions." Standing in front of a shining metal surface or caldron, grieving ancients saw and spoke with familiar apparitions. The Sumerians, Egyptians, and Romans employed similar oracles of polished crystal, brass mirrors, and pools of water. Some believe the Apostle Paul was referring to a mirror-oracle when he said, "For now we see through a glass, darkly; but then face to face:

now I know in part; but then shall I know even as also I am known" (1 Cor. 13.12).

Psychomanteums today are used to facilitate contact with ETs, deities, and deceased relatives or family members. Various versions of Psychomanteums are even encouraged by some psychiatrists as a method for dealing with grief. Sometimes under special (nefarious?) conditions, the mirror-contact phenomenon spontaneously occurs. As a teenager, my wife was involved in a horrific accident that killed her dad and sister. Following the accident, her eleven-year-old sister "materialized" in the bedroom mirror on two occasions. Since the house she lived in was formerly occupied by an unusual band of gypsies, my wife believed this fact contributed to the spontaneous Psychomanteum activity.

In their book *Reunions* by Raymond Moody and Paul Perry, Raymond Moody promotes the use of Psychomanteums as oracles. He documents the experiences of more than three hundred users of the device and points out that 50 percent claimed to have been contacted by entities or deceased relatives and friends during the first try.

People interviewed by Mr. Moody include physicians, teachers, housewives, business owners, and law enforcement officials. One such witness, an accountant that grieved over his departed mother a year after her death, testifies of his experience with the Psychomanteum:

> There is no doubt that the person I saw in the mirror was my mother! I don't know where she came from but I am convinced that what I saw was the real person. She was looking out at me from the mirror...I could tell she was in her late 70s, about the same age as...when she died. However, she looked happier and healthier than

she had at the end of her life. Her lips didn't move, but she spoke to me and I clearly heard what she had to say. She said, "I'm fine," and smiled...I stayed as relaxed as I could and just looked at her...Then I decided to talk to her. I said, "It's good to see you again." "It's good to see you too," she replied. That was it. She simply disappeared. (Moody 54-62)

A physician was unexpectedly contacted by a nephew while seated in a psychomanteum:

I suddenly had a very strong sense of the presence of my nephew, who had committed suicide...I heard his voice very clearly. He greeted me and brought me a very simple message. He said, "Let my mother know that I am fine and that I love her very much." This experience was profound. I know he was there with me. (Moody 54-62)

Although the Bible warns of communicating with familiar spirits, consulting mediums, or otherwise offering invitations to other-dimensional entities, the revival of ancient oracles and the experiences drawn from them are especially seductive curiosities to followers of modern Ufology and spiritualism. Communications with deities, ETs, the dead, channeling, trancing, near-death experiences, and other forms of mediumship, harmonize a coveted and reassuring theme, "You are not alone in the universe," or "I'm fine now," "All is well," "I'm waiting for you."

Jacques Vallée offers tantalizing clues to the identity of those behind this veil:

...should we hypothesize that an advanced race somewhere in the universe in some time in the future has been showing us three-dimensional space operas for the last 2000 years, in an attempt to guide our civilization? If so, do they deserve congratulations?...Are we dealing instead with a parallel universe, another dimension, where there are human races living, and where we may go at our expense, never to return to the present? Are these races only semi-human, so that in order to maintain contact with us, they need cross-breeding with men and woman of our planet? Is this the origin of the many tales and legends where genetics play a great role:...the fairy tales involving human midwives and changelings, the sexual overtones of the flying saucer reports, the Biblical stories of intermarriage between the Lord's angels and terrestrial women, whose offspring were giants? From that mysterious universe are higher beings projecting objects that can materialize and dematerialize at will? (Vallée 143-144)

Materializing and dematerializing of superintelligent beings, whether angels or ETs, is not difficult to accept. The Bible, as well as other ancient records, speak openly of Satan appearing as an angel of light, and of good angels hosted as "angels unaware" (Heb. 13.2). We also are willing to believe that malevolent beings could produce UFOs for nefarious reasons. The theology of transmogrification, whereby spirits take form, indicates ability by demons to manipulate energy/matter. The German word "poltergeist" was given to explain spirit noises and/or activity, and if "spirits" actually cause audible vibrations, they have ability to make physical contact with tangible materials, to manipulate atomic structures at some level. This being theologically acceptable, maybe Vallée is right about historical "demons" producing phenomena known as UFOs—the manifested manipulating of vital energy—in order to construct a gateway from one dimension to another.

Vallée continues:

> Are we dealing instead with a parallel universe...From that mysterious universe, have objects that can materialize and "dematerialize" at will been projected? Are the UFOs "windows" [stargates] rather than "objects"? (153-154)

TRANSGENIC PSYCHOTRONICS

The use of "vital energy" by ultraterrestrials to form dimensional gateways—whether by manipulating animal, plant, or atmospheric molecular energy—brings interesting questions to the biblical story of Genesis, where some believe superintelligent angels known as "Watchers" descended to earth and used antediluvian cell matter, including women, animals, and plants to construct for themselves "portals," through which they extended themselves into the material world, bringing with them physical and psychotronic warfare.

Note the implication behind this activity in Genesis, "The benei Elohim saw the daughters of Adam, that they were fit extensions" (Interlinear Hebrew Bible, Gen. 6.2). "Fit extensions" could be understood to mean portals (stargates) or the use of molecular energy to format navigational dimensional pathways. Current advances by modern scientists to blend DNA of various species using biotechnology (such as transgenics to genetically modify crops, create mice with human brains, goats with human blood, and animal-human hybrids for medical research) raise a host of prophetic possibilities and questions in light of Genesis 6:

- Apocryphal books such as Enoch, 2 Esdras, Genesis Aprocryphon, Jasher and others expand the Genesis story to reveal that the "sin" of angels with women included similar simultaneous activity against nature, animals, and plants. For instance the Book of Jasher, which is mentioned in the Bible in Joshua 10.13 and 2 Samuel 1.18, says, "After the fallen angels went into the daughters of men, [then] the sons of men taught the mixture of animals of one species with the other, in order to provoke the Lord" (4.18). This clear reference to the Genesis 6 record adds "animals" to the cross-species experiments that sought to alter creation from divine order and which resulted in judgment from God. The Book of Enoch says the fallen angels not only merged their DNA with women but that "they began to sin against birds, and beasts, and reptiles, and fish" (7.5; 6). The Old Testament contains many references to the genetic oddities that developed among men following the creation of Nephilim, including unusual size, physical strength, six fingers, six toes, and even lionlike features (2 Sam. 21.20; 23.20)!

- The reason "Watchers" might have been transgenically blending *their* species with human DNA as well as animal and plant DNA (various living organisms) remains a mystery, but it is curiously compelling in light of *modern* transgenic and similar well-funded research. Are we seeing the fulfillment of prophecy? "As it was in the days of Noah..." (Luke 17.26)?

- Equally important are the two-fold parts of the Genesis 6 story: 1) Mature women were used (changed/altered?) to become fit extensions or acceptable hosts for the Watchers. Is this what was happening in Genesis 10 concerning Nimrod when "...*he began [khaw-lal* (a word study here is enlightening as the verb indicates the "beginning" of profaning oneself or defiling oneself either sexually or ritually—exactly what some scholars believe the Watchers did to humans and animals in the lead up to Nephilim)] *to be [become] a **mighty*** [Gibbowr (of which we derive Gibborim/Nephilim)] *one in the earth*"? This text could be read, "Nimrod began to become a Nephilim" or "a child of the Nephilim." Is this a record of a mature human agreeing to be altered at the genetic level?; 2) The offspring of this genetic alteration was "resurrected" dead Nephilim. Note the rendering, "...**afterward** [after the flood] when the benei Elohim came in to the daughters of Adam, and they bore to them—**they** [the newly born Nephilim] were Powerful Ones which **existed from ancient times** [pre-existed or were alive once before the flood], the men of name" [emphasis added] (Interlinear Hebrew Bible, Gen. 6.4).

The most enlightening, corresponding evidence of the assertion above is found in the historical relationship between the Nephilim and the Rephaim, or spirits of dead Nephilim. Rephaim carries with it the meaning "to heal" or to be "healed" as in a "resurrection." In the Ras Shamra texts, the Rephaim are described as both human and divine beings who worshipped the Amorite god Ba'al, the ruler of the underworld, where the Rephaim served as his acolyte assembly of lesser gods, kings, heroes, and rulers. These beings were believed to have power to return from the dead through incarnation in bodily form as gods or "Nephilim."

The book of Job elucidates this idea in relation to the

Nephilim when it says, "Dead things are formed from under the waters…." (Job 26.5). The *dead* in this text are Rapha and the phrase *are formed* is from "Chuwl," meaning to twist or whirl (as in a double helix coil or genetic manufacturing). When combined with something my good friend Steve Quayle once wrote, the word "Chuwl" takes on added meaning:

> When the Greek Septuagint was created, the Hebrew word Nephilim was translated into Greek as "gegenes." This is the same word used in Greek mythology for the "Titans," creatures created through the interbreeding of the Greek gods and human beings. The English words "genes" and "genetics" are built around the same root word as gegenes, genea meaning "breed" or "kind." Thus, the choice of this word again suggests a genetic component to the creation of these giants. (Quayle 128)

The idea that the spirits of dead giants inhabit the underworld is also supported in the following texts:

- "They're segregated from the heroes, the old time giants who entered [hell] in full battle dress…" (The Message Version, Ezekiel 32.27).
- "And he did not know that giants are there, and that her guests are in the depths of hell" (Douay-Rheims Version, Proverbs 9.18).
- "A man that shall wander out of the way of doctrine, shall abide in the company of the giants" (Douay-Rheims, Version Proverbs 21.16).
- "Hell below was in an uproar to meet thee at thy coming, it stirred up the giants for thee" (Douay-Rheims Version, Isaiah 14.9).

- "Let not the dead live, let not the giants rise again..." (Douay-Rheims Version, Isaiah 26.14).

This last reference above is very important to the remainder of this book, as it actually reflects a prayer from the prophet, a petition to God not to allow the giants to incarnate again. As we shall see later, I believe Isaiah prayed this way because he knew something about the future, something related to portals...and the giants who are prophesied to come through them at the end of time.

Such information also raises astonishing speculation, which may supply additional reasoning behind the terror that ancient men had of Nephilim.

What if, by corrupting the species "barrier" commanded by God in which each creature was to recreate after its "own kind," Watchers had successfully mingled human-animal-plant DNA and combined the hereditary traits of several species into a single new mutation? An entirely new being—Nephilim—might have suddenly possessed the combined intelligence and instincts (seeing, hearing, smelling, reacting to the environment, etc.) of several life forms and in ways unfamiliar to ancient men.

WILL MODERN BIOTECHNOLOGY PLAY A ROLE IN THE RETURN OF NEPHILIM?

Today, molecular biologists classify the functions of genes within native species but are unsure in many cases how a gene's coding might react from one species to another. In recombinant DNA technology, a "transgenic" organism is created when the genetic structure of one species is altered by the transfer of a gene or genes from another. This could change not only the genetic structure of the modified animal and its offspring, but its evolutionary development, sensory modalities, disease propensity, personality, behavior traits, and more.

Such transgenic tinkering already exists in many parts of the world, including the United States, Britain, and Australia where animal eggs are being used to create hybrid human embryos from which stem cell lines can be produced for medical research. A team at Newcastle and Durham universities in the UK recently announced plans to "create hybrid rabbit and human embryos, as well as other 'chimera' embryos mixing human and cow genes" (Picken). More alarmingly, the same researchers have already managed to reanimate tissue "from dead human cells in another breakthrough which was heralded as a way of overcoming ethical dilemmas over using living embryos for medical research" (Picken). In the United States, similar studies led Irv Weissman, director of Stanford University's Institute of Cancer/Stem Cell Biology and Medicine in California to create mice with partly human brains, causing some ethicists to raise the issue of "humanized animals" in the future that could become "self aware" as a result of genetic modification. Even the President of the United States, George W. Bush in his January 31, 2006 State of the Union Address called for legislation to "prohibit...creating human-animal hybrids, and buying, selling, or patenting human embryos."

Not everybody shares these concerns. A radical, international, intellectual, and cultural movement known as "Transhumanism" supports the use of new sciences, including genetic modification to enhance human mental and physical abilities and aptitudes, so that "human beings will eventually be transformed into beings with such greatly expanded abilities as to merit the label 'posthuman'" (Wikipedia, Transhumanism).

I have personally debated leading transhumanist, Dr. James Hughes on his weekly syndicated talk show, *Changesurfer*

Radio. Hughes is Executive Director of the Institute for Ethics and Emerging Technologies and teaches at Trinity College in Hartford Connecticut. He is also the author of *Citizen Cyborg: Why Democratic Societies Must Respond to the Redesigned Human of the Future*, a sort of Bible for transhumanist values. Dr. Hughes joins a growing body of academics, bioethicists and sociologists who support large-scale genetic and neurological engineering of ourselves...[a] new chapter in evolution [as] the result of accelerating developments in the fields of genomics, stem-cell research, genetic enhancement, germ-line engineering, neuro-pharmacology, artificial intelligence, robotics, pattern recognition technologies, and nanotechnology...at the intersection of science and religion [which has begun to question] what it means to be human...(Grassie)

In related development, Case Law School in Cleveland was awarded a $773,000 grant in April 2006 from the National Institutes of Health to develop guidelines "for the use of human subjects in what could be the next frontier in medical technology—genetic enhancement." Maxwell Mehlman, Arthur E. Petersilge Professor of Law, director of the Law-Medicine Center at the Case Western Reserve University School of Law, and professor of bioethics in the Case School of Medicine is leading the team of law professors, physicians, and bioethicists in the two-year project to develop standards for tests on human subjects in research that involves the use of genetic technologies to enhance "normal" individuals—to make them smarter, stronger, or better-looking. (Case Western Reserve University).

Other law schools including Stanford and Oxford have recently hosted "Human Enhancement and Technology" conferences where transhumanists, futurists, bioethicists and legal scholars merged to discuss the ethical and legal ramifications of posthumans.

In his book *Life, Liberty and the Defense of Dignity: The Challenges of Bioethics*, the former chairman of the President's Council on Bioethics, Leon Kass provides a status report on where we stand today regarding transhumanism. He warns in the introduction that Human nature itself lies on the operating table, ready for alteration, for eugenic and psychic "enhancement," for wholesale redesign. In leading laboratories, academic and industrial, new creators are confidently amassing their powers and quietly honing their skills, while on the street their evangelists are zealously prophesying a posthuman future. For anyone who cares about preserving our humanity, the time has come for paying attention. (Kass, Introduction)

Not to be outdone in this regard by the National Institute of Health, DARPA and other agencies of the US military have taken inspiration from the likes of Tolkein's *Lord of the Rings*. In a scene reminiscent of Saruman the wizard creating monstrous Uruk-Hai to wage unending, merciless war, we find billions of American tax dollars have flowed into the Pentagon's Frankensteinian dream of "super-soldiers" and the "Extended Performance War Fighter" program. Not only does the EPWFP envision injecting young men and women with hormonal, neurological and genetic concoctions; implanting microchips and electrodes in their bodies to control their internal organs and brain functions; and plying them with drugs that deaden some of their normal human tendencies: the need for sleep, the fear of death, [and] the reluctance to kill their fellow human beings, (Floyd) but Chris Floyd in an article for *CounterPunch* a while back quoted the *Daily Telegraph* and *Christian Science Monitor*, saying:

some of the research now underway involves actually altering the genetic code of soldiers, modifying bits of

DNA to fashion a new type of human specimen, one that functions like a machine, killing tirelessly for days and nights on end...mutations [that] will "revolutionize the contemporary order of battle" and guarantee "operational dominance across the whole range of potential US military employments." (Floyd)

In keeping with our study, imagine the staggering implications of such science if dead Nephilim tissue were discovered with intact DNA and there were a government somewhere that were willing to clone or mingle the extracted organisms to make Homo-Nephilim. If one accepts the biblical story of giants as real, such discovery could actually be made someday, or perhaps already has been and was covered up. The technology to resurrect the extinct species already exists, and cloning methods are being studied now for use with bringing back Tasmanian Tigers, Wooly Mammoths, and other extinguished creatures.

What would the ramifications of animal-human-Nephilim be? Multitude. For instance, animals can "sense" earthquakes and "smell" tumors. Some of them, like dogs, can hear sounds as high as 40,000 Hz, and dolphins can hear even higher. It is also known some animals see wavelengths of the electromagnetic spectrum beyond human ability. As our understanding of quantum physics, including light and dark matter, expands, we may come to more fully appreciate the Bible's references to beings of "light" and beings of "darkness" and one more thing—that some animals "see" *spirits*. The Bible provides verification for this in the story of Balaam's donkey. Modern researchers likewise have uncovered evidence that animals often seem to react to things *unseen*. Have you ever seen a dog barking or growling at "nothing"?

Now imagine what this could mean if government laboratories with unlimited budgets working beyond congressional review were to decode the gene functions that lead to animal propensities of sense, smell, sight. The ultimate psychotronic warfare could be committed against entire populations by "agents" who appear to be human but who see and even interact with invisible forces. Biblical and apocryphal texts indicate such may have been the case with Nephilim and bring an entirely new context to the fear-factor ancient men had of these beings. Yet, this terrifying example is only the tip of the iceberg. If interbreeding between regular and transgenic humans (a possibility many believe not only explains Genesis 6 but that could point to an imminent possibility, given modern science and man's tendency to throw caution to the wind when given the chance to play "god") ever occurs, mutated DNA will get out of the bottle. When and if that happens, "alien" and/or animal characteristics will be introduced to the human species, altering the human genetic code and eventually eliminating humanity as we know it. Such was certainly the goal of Adolf Hitler, as noted in *The Dawn of Magic* by Louis Pauwells & Jacques Bergier (first published in France under the title "Le Matin des Magiciens" 1960 by Editions Gallimard, Paris):

Hitler's aim was neither the founding of a race of supermen, nor the conquest of the world; these were only means towards the realization of the great work he dreamed of. His real aim was to perform an act of creation, a divine operation, the goal of a biological mutation which would result in an unprecedented exaltation of the human race and the "apparition of a new race of heroes and demigods and god-men" (Louis).

Some believe that was (Gen 6), and could be again, the whole idea.

1. Holography

In addition to hypothetical manipulation of "vital energy" for creating "portals," stargate manipulators could employ holographic projections or holography, the method of producing and broadcasting three-dimensional images to create the illusion of traversing multi-dimensions. When I asked Dr. Steven M. Greer, the director of The Disclosure Project (which has over 450 military, government and corporate insiders who claim first-hand knowledge of actual UFO/ET events) to clarify a statement he made recently that members of his team "have interacted with these UFOs—and with the beings on-board them" (Greer). Greer clarified, "Tom, CSETI has conducted expeditions around the world and has encountered hundreds of UFOs in interactive events, including interactions with what appear to be holographic type projections of ET beings in or near the CSETI groups." Though Greer's groups are known to invite such experiences, my niece a few years ago may have had a similar, albeit uninvited other-dimensional holography from an unknown intelligence. She is a federal employee and trained analyst for the Social Security Division. She also is what the UFO community calls an "experiencer" or abductee, as is her mother. She has spoken privately with the chief medical examiner and the head psychiatrist at the SSD concerning her sanity, and incredibly they assured her that she is sane, and that "...aliens and [her] experiences are real." (Later we shall discuss how prayer creates a firewall between her and this activity, illustrating what I believe to be proof of the spiritual aspects of the so-called alien abduction phenomenon.)

My niece has a streaming-camera on her computer that allows her to send images back and forth as she communicates with friends via the Internet. One night as she was chatting with friends, a frame popped onto her computer that appeared to be showing a 'creature' standing at one side and behind her. What looked like an unknown being was half inside the frame, its slender thin arm extending downward, while a reddish, preying mantis-like eye was observing her. When my niece spun around, nothing was there. The experience terrified her so much that I agreed to have the photo analyzed by a leading expert. His conclusion was that the image is not a fake and that an unknown light source might have been creating the anomaly. Another expert examined the image following an interview I did with George Noory on *Coast to Coast AM*, and his finding was also that the image is not a fake. His analysis showed additional details including what appear to be fingers. Was this an example of alien holography or other advanced method used by superintelligences to manipulate light photons or otherwise create three-dimensional expressions? Holography? The case is still out.

2. Wormholes as Stargates

Besides holography and the possible manipulation of "vital energy," recent improvements in our understanding of general relativity has caused some to believe stargate manipulators could "appear" and "disappear" through traversable wormholes. Alan Holt first defined the "field resonance space-time tunneling" in 1979, or what today is more commonly called "wormholes" or "stargates." The theory is that hyperspace tunnels may connect: (a) remote regions of universes and/or; (b) different dimensions and/or; (c) different moments in time. UFOs could hypothetically travel through these space-time tunnels from incredibly far distances to the earth in matters of seconds or maybe even at speeds *greater than light!*

In his presentation at the MUFON International UFO Symposium in July, 2001, Dr. Eric W. Davies said:

> The craft seen during UFO encounters would likely be exploiting wormholes in order to intersect with our local space and interact with us, and the intelligence that controls wormhole technology could also use them as a window to peer into and probe our world without having to send craft through . . . Wormhole-stargates could essentially facilitate the manifestation of phenomenon in our world by acting as a doorway through which UFOs would visit us from other universes, dimensions or space-time. (Davies)

Wormholes as stargates would explain some of the observations made by eyewitness of UFOs suddenly appearing and disappearing and even gradually vanishing. Other elements consistent with theoretical and known laws of advanced and quantum physics would make sense as well, such as "booming sounds" when UFOs pass through dimensional portals. Only now are scientists beginning to understand the advanced methods ultraterrestrials could be employing to travel through universes and time in the blink of our three-dimensional eye. Interestingly, many suspected that such methods of hyperspace travel was possible even before the theorem provided for it. In 1974, Alan Landsburg and Sally Landsburg wrote in their book, *In Search of Ancient Mysteries*:

> In New York are two apartment buildings, back to back. The entrance to one in on Fifth Avenue, the entrance to

the other on Sixth. Mr. White and his wife live on the seventh floor of one of those buildings. A wall of their living room is the back wall of the building.

Their friends the Blacks live on the seventh floor of the other building, and a wall of their living room is the back wall of their building. So these two couples live within two feet of each other, since the back building walls actually touch. But, of course, they don't see or hear each other.

When the Blacks want to visit the Whites, they walk from their living room to the front door. Then they walk down a long hall to the elevator. They ride seven floors down. Then, in the street, they must walk around to the next block - and the city blocks are long. In bad weather they must sometimes actually take a cab. They walk into the other building, they go through the lobby, ride up seven floors, walk down a hall, ring a bell, and finally enter their friend's living room—only two feet from their own.

The way the Blacks travel is like our civilization's space travel—the actual physical crossing of enormous three-dimensional spaces. But if they could only step through those two feet of wall without harming themselves or the wall—well, maybe that's how the old ones come here from their mysterious planet" (Landsburg 185).

Chapter 10

LEVIATHAN
AMONG US

Researchers working at the Human Genome Project may soon announce an astonishing scientific conclusion: So-called non-coding sequences (97%) in human DNA is no less than the genetic code of an unknown extraterrestrial life form (Stokes). Some believe this may establish yet another step toward Official Disclosure and certainly the potential for a ferocious debate among members of science and religious communities concerning the origin of Homo Sapiens. Speculation exists—it is said—that "hidden codes" in "junk DNA" may be deciphered in an as-yet unknown dialect potentially describing facts about the creation of mankind and further astounding discoveries on the event-horizon in what now appears to be a countdown toward the end of the age and the re-opening of portals of air, earth, great rivers, and sea.

The Great Deception.

COUNTDOWN: THE RETURN
OF MAN'S CREATOR

Earliest histories from around the world speak of significant involvement by "superintelligences" involved in the origin of the species with promises by this Creator to return someday. Secular and religious Ufologists point to the universal documentation of such history as a record of "heavenly beings" visiting earth and engaging in a process leading to hominid creation and the first civilizations. When the Sumerians first appeared, following the event described above, they brought with them a pantheon of sky deities, the first written language, and a superior knowledge of the cosmos. Post Sumerian myth held that powerful beings with names like "Zeus" and "Apollo" visited the earth, intermarried with women, and fathered half-human children. In 1986, Christian college professor I.D.E. Thomas combined this mythos with modern Ufology, claiming that a race of anti-God warriors were approaching the earth from "out there" and were bringing with them end-times delusion and Armageddon. Evangelical apologists since have flooded the marketplace with dire warnings of a false Messiah who, they say, will appear "in the heavens" in the last days to set about deceiving the world.

Whereas Ufologists of various creeds disagree on the meaning of particular ET phenomenon, the main camps assert language that define UFOs and extraterrestrial intelligence in angeological and demonological terms, including promises by the Creator to return through heaven's "gates" at the end of time. Some hold therefore that religious and non-religious Ufologists are saying the same thing but from different points of view. Most religions have at least one apocalyptic myth describing the end of the world accompanied by a "savior" who appears in the sky at the last minute to rescue the "chosen" from annihilation or wrath.

Sumerians, Mayans, Assyrians, Egyptians, and Greeks held similar beliefs. Hopi prophecy talks of a time of great destruction, when their lands will be preserved when "a blue star, far off and invisible, makes its appearance." Even factions of the modern New Age look for a techno-savior to appear in the clouds to save mankind from itself.

Yet if man's Creator is about to return and the available evidence—including universal historical records—is interpreted differently by separate schools of thought, it is important to summarize the interpretive difference of the two main bodies of belief—the biblical (Christian) and extra-biblical (secular).

Predominant among some church scholars is the idea that coupled with any heavenly appearing of a superintelligence will be the materialization of a false Christ or "man of sin." This is a line in the sand for many Christians, dividing them from persons of different faiths who also look to the skies for redemption. Whereas Hopi see a blue star, and others see returning ancient astronauts, Christians worry that any belief not consistent with their own might open a door for Antichrist to assume the role of a false Messiah by mimicking the return of Christ. Nowhere is the conflict regarding the imminent appearing of a descending savior more glaring than among Christian and secular Ufologists. While some on both sides resist combining religious and cosmological significance with Extraterrestrial Intelligence (Vatican officials have gone so far recently as to release a series of calculated responses meant to reassure Catholics that evidence of ET or sudden visitation by such would not prove "everything we believe in is wrong," rather, "we're going to find out that everything is truer in ways we couldn't even yet have imagined," [Glatz]), others hold to the opposite position, esoterically and biblically.

Hal Lindsey states, "I have become thoroughly convinced

that UFOs are real…I believe these beings are not only extra-terrestrial but supernatural in origin. To be blunt, I think they are demons" (Lindsey 68). In *Angels Dark and Light*, Gary Kinnaman agrees, "I am fairly convinced that…UFO sightings are the manifestations of angels of darkness. My main reason for thinking this is that UFO sightings have never, at least to my knowledge, led a person closer to God. In fact, most UFO experiences have just the opposite effect" (Kinnaman 132-133).

To men such as these, it is easy to believe that demons are involved with "flying saucers." According to such theology, "evil spirits" can manipulate energy and matter, and the theological terms, "Transmogrification" and "Poltergeist" ("noisy ghost"), imply that spirits make lights go off and on, doors bang, and saucers fly. Yet if a portion of "flying saucer" activity is demonic, what nefarious purpose is served by the stealthy nature of UFO phenomenon? The answer, they say, is diabolical.

UFO-ism according to many Christians seems to be aimed at preparing the earth for an extraterrestrial "visitation of the gods," and, more importantly, at changing the world's religious beliefs. This would occur in two ways First, from a technological standpoint, UFO sightings challenge the claim of human superiority and dispute man's unique role in the universe. We are made to feel shallow, undeveloped, unenlightened in our world and cosmological view, when it is Christian. Second, extraterrestrials offer a message (as reported in hundreds of abduction cases) of easy universalism and New Age mysticism including dialogue of humans on the verge of extraordinary telepathic and technological growth. The "benevolent ETs" profess to watch over us and promise to appear at the appropriate time to assist us in our next evolutionary, spiritual, and technological step forward. To prepare us for their coming, popular movies, bestselling books, cultural trends, and religious ideas focus the earth's masses on "help from above," while supporters smile and explain "It's okay, they've been here before" and "Don't worry, ancient men simply described flying saucers in terms of demons, angels, and gods, because they didn't understand what they were seeing."

In other words, space vehicles manipulating known laws of physics (suddenly appearing and disappearing, operating anti-gravitationally, etc.) were assigned "god" or "angel" status by sincere but ignorant prophets, and Ezekiel's living creatures will return soon in their wheels "in the middle of a wheel" providing true explanations of themselves, our origin, and solutions to our problems.

In what may be a prophecy of end-time UFOs, Isaiah connected the benei Elohim to "fiery flying seraph." We read:

> Do not rejoice O Philistia, all of you, for the rod of your striking is broken, because a viper [Antichrist?] comes forth from the root of the snake [Satan?] and his fruit is the fiery flying seraph. (Is. 14.29)

This descriptive language is amazing given the predominant and universal citations of flying serpent "gods" and the promises of their return in the heavens at the end of time. The seraph (seraphim) were powerful angels known for their brilliance, some of which may have followed Lucifer in the fall. Are such "fiery flying seraph" the source of UFOs today? If alien "angels" appeared in the days before the flood performing genetic experiments on the daughters of Adam and producing mutant Nephilim, does the prophecy of Jesus in Luke 17.26 forecast such activity as reoccurring at the end of time? Similar questions asked by Christian Ufologists include: Does recent UFO abduction activity point to genetic engineering of a new race of anti-God warriors (Nephilim) as we approach a Great Tribulation? Will "UFOs" provide a grand entry for the ultimate cross-mutation of angelic and human species—the god-king of the New World Order?

In *Mythology: A Visual Encyclopedia*, Jo Forty says something interesting with regard to this—that the Antichrist was viewed by the early church not only as a forthcoming tyrant, "but also... *as having flight capability*" [emphasis added] (Forty 250). Why would "flight capability" be associated with the Antichrist? Was a "galactic battle" known to have occurred that tied together in the minds of ancients the idea that "gods" fought it out in the heavens and that, more importantly, a future War of the Worlds would be fought again between these celestial powers? Between a Creator God and false creators?

Some may be surprised to learn that a return of the flying gods of mythology is clearly described in biblical end times prophecies. The "old gods" (Zeus, Apollo, Demeter, Isis?) are viewed as going to war with God during the last days. Yet "The Lord will be terrible unto them: for he will famish all the gods" (Zeph. 2.11), and "The Lord of hosts, the God of Israel, saith; Behold, I will punish the...gods" (Jer. 46.25). Most significantly, the Bible describes the Almighty as punishing the leader of these gods—"that old serpent, called the Devil."

WHEN GODS AND
DRAGONS COME THROUGH PORTALS

Around the world an interesting story is repeated about "the god" of heaven warring with "the dragon" of the sea during both the beginning and ending of time. The earliest versions of this story date back to Sumerian and Hebrew sources. Unlike Sumerian text, in the book of Job there is reference not only to Cetus, the Sea Monster, and Draco, but clear description of Leviathan—the Great Dragon of the sea:

> Canst thou draw out leviathan with an hook? or his tongue with a cord which thou lettest down?…Canst thou fill his skin with barbed irons? or his head with fish spears?…Who can discover the face of his garment? or who can come to him with his double bridle?…Who can open the doors of his face? his teeth are terrible round about. His scales are his pride, shut up together as with a close seal. One is so near to another, that no air can come between them. They are joined one to another, they stick together, that they cannot be sundered. By his neesings a light doth shine, and his eyes are like the eyelids of the morning. Out of his mouth go burning lamps, and sparks of fire leap out. Out of his nostrils goeth smoke, as out of a seething pot or caldron. His breath kindleth coals, and a flame goeth out of his mouth. In his neck remaineth strength, and sorrow is turned into joy before him. The flakes of his flesh are joined together: they are firm in themselves; they cannot be moved. His heart is as firm as a stone; yea, as hard as a piece of the nether millstone. When he raiseth up himself, the mighty are afraid: by reason of breakings they purify themselves. The sword of him that layeth at him cannot hold: the spear, the dart, nor the habergeon. He esteemeth iron as straw, and brass as rotten wood. The arrow cannot make him flee: slingstones are turned with him into stubble. Darts are counted as stubble: he laugheth at the shaking of a spear. Sharp stones are under him: he spreadeth sharp pointed things upon the

mire. He maketh the deep to boil like a pot: he maketh the sea like a pot of ointment. He maketh a path to shine after him; one would think the deep to be hoary. Upon earth there is not his like, who is made without fear. He beholdeth all high things: he is a king over all the children of pride." (Job 41.1-34)

In what may be the oldest book in all of human history, we find abundant physical details of the Great Dragon in the sea who is the king of "all the children of pride" (Lucifer/Satan) and who cannot be mastered by any other than God alone. In the litanies of the witches' Sabbath, this Leviathan is ranked, together with Lucifer and Baalzebub, as an equal member of the supreme trinity of evil. Bible prophecy indicates final conflict between God and this Dragon as unfinished business which resumes at the end of time. Therefore, according to Scripture, a powerful spirit—literally a dragon—lurks beneath the waters (or is bound in the great seas) awaiting a future time (a gate opening?) when final conflict will be engaged between itself and the Creator God.

In Isaiah, we read of this:

Come, my people, enter thou into thy chambers, and shut thy doors about thee: hide thyself as it were for a little moment, until the indignation be overpast. For, behold, the Lord cometh out of his place to punish the inhabitants of the earth for their iniquity: the earth also shall disclose her blood, and shall no more cover her slain. In that day the Lord with his sore and great and strong sword shall punish Leviathan the piercing serpent, even Leviathan that crooked serpent; and he shall slay the dragon that is in the sea. (Is. 26.20-27.1)

PRECONDITIONING FOR
THE FINAL CONFLICT, OR GIANT HOAX?

Recently a story we avoided at *RaidersNewsNetwork.com* but that flourished elsewhere on the web told of a giant Leviathan-type creature discovered in the polar ice of Franz Josef Land. The colossal being was described as having horns *"immense in dimension"* that protruded from its head "with incredible length. The body is covered with a combination of coarse fur and what can best be described as 'body armor' (like an American armadillo)—protects its enormous joints and head" (Ice).

The story included video and audio reports. Our friend Steve Quayle of the "Q-Files" did some investigative work and after talking to the helicopter pilot in the Leviathan Video, determined it was a fake. He reported his findings to George Noory that same week on Coast to Coast AM. Sony evidently had hired a team to create a docudrama for a new Playstation 2 game called, "Shadow of the Colossus."

Or *is* that what happened? Further research suggests this could have been a cover up, a bait-and-switch, designed to throw people off the trail of legitimate recovery efforts at or near the Franz Josef site. During RaidersNewsNetwork's own investigative research, we found several interesting and potentially telling pieces of the puzzle, not the least of which involved P.J. Capelotti—senior lecturer in anthropology and American studies at Penn State University Abington College in Abington—who had conducted archaeological studies of Franz Josef Land (where the hoax was perpetuated). Capelotti followed his research of the site with a suspect thesis on the need to establish international laws and/or treaties to *preserve alien artifacts!*

Among other things, Capelotti points out that the late biochemist and science fiction writer Isaac Asimov once speculated that the galaxy may contain 325 million planets with traces of civilizations in ruins. Perhaps our astronomers and their SETI stations are hearing only static through their radio telescopes because they are, in effect, listening for a message from the extraterrestrial equivalent of the ancient Maya or the Sumerians—dead civilizations that can speak to us now only through archaeology. Constructing a catalog of visual signatures of advanced civilizations will someday be within the province of aerospace archaeology. And with a potential cultural resource database of 325 million planets with civilizations in ruins, there sure is a lot of fieldwork to do 'out there.'" (Capelotti)

Did Capelotti's team discover something in Franz Josef Land and/or nearby expedition sites needing international protection... something that corresponds to artificial remains elsewhere in the galaxy that also needs international protection...something big enough to, let's say, employ Sony to concoct a cover-up? As extraordinary as that sounds, history proves repeatedly that governments have participated in similar scenarios on more than one occasion. A few years ago, Disney worked with an army of NASA scientists, astronauts, and technicians to produce the film "Mission to Mars." The story sent NASA Commander Luke Graham (Don Cheadle) with a crew of four astronauts to the red planet. While exploring strange geological formations on the landscape, the truth about the Face on Mars and the origin of mankind was discovered. At the time, director Brian De Palma admitted, "*Mission to Mars* is set in 2020 because that's the date the experts predict we should have a manned landing on Mars." Soon a row reportedly took place between NASA and Disney, as it seemed the agency didn't like what the film was insinuating: that a discovery had been made of past alien presence on Mars, that an artificial Sphinx-like "face" and pyramidal shapes near it (photographed by the Viking Mars probe) had been discovered, and a twenty-five-year cover-up had been per-petrated by NASA and the US Government in collusion with other world powers.

It is impossible to know where the smoke begins and ends with stories like these, so we stick with the inspired texts. They tell us of creation and of the future return of the Creator. War between this Almighty and the gods who come through gate-ways will occur. "They" will come from air, earth, great rivers, and from the bottom of the sea. There is no way to avoid that moment in time.

John Milton wrote in *Paradise Lost* that millions of spiritual creatures walk the earth unseen. The biblical view, as postulated in my book *The Gods Who Walk Among Us*, affirms the idea that "In the beginning" Yahweh created the heavens (celestial beings, planets, etc.) and the earth. Lucifer, "the light bearer," was a crowning achievement of God's heavenly creation and a chief servant of the creative Yahweh. Yet according to the story, Lucifer became jealous of the worship Yahweh was receiving from his many creations, and proudly proclaimed, "I will exalt my throne above the stars of God.... I will be like the most high" (Is.14.13-14). Somehow Lucifer convinced one-third of the celestial creatures to join him in great rebellion, with the uprising ultimately resulting in Lucifer and his followers being cast out of heaven. Lucifer (now Satan), driven by a quest for worship and thirsty for revenge with Yahweh, tempted Eve and, after the fall with its resulting separation between man and God, moved to corrupt the divine truths contained within the Original Revelation by proclaiming himself (the god of the air) more worthy of worship than was the God of heaven.

If such an assumption of the biblical view is correct—that a real and evil supernatural presence exists and has for centu-ries drawn men away from worshipping Yahweh through the dynamics of various mythologies—the following questions arise: Were the angels that joined Lucifer in the fall also driven by a lust for worship? Did the images and attributes ascribed to the gods of mythology somehow reflect the real and spiritual characteristics of certain unseen personalities operating behind them? More importantly, is the kingdom of Satan still at work in this manner? Do the living entities of ancient gods continue to pass through portals, to walk among us? If so, do such spirits embody themselves in trees, earth, and idols of stone, or should we assume modern idolatry has acquired a more selective sophistication and social manifestation, one that has in this century brought clearer detail to their *gray* image?

Chapter 11

MORE FICTION? THE BREEDING EXPERIMENT PLAYED OUT

ronically, I am writing chapter 11 of this book during the 11th month of the year. In other words, 11.11. I have at times felt a strange sense of destiny during the inspirational moments of *Nephilim Stargates: The Year 2012 and the Return of the Watchers,* as though an invisible hand were guiding me. Yet for some reason I had not noticed before now that the timing of my pace corresponds to the most important day of the Mayan calendar (as a Christian, I refer to the synchronicity of Mayan prophecy and complex knowledge of astronomy as noteworthy to this study), the end-date of December 21, 2012, at exactly 11:11—when the Winter Solstice and the Galactic Equinox occurs and the Solar System aligns with the center of the Galaxy. This event happens only every 25,000 years, and this time it marks the end of the great Mayan Calendar and the moment when Mayan prophecy says

Quetzalcoatl will return through a stargate in a winged (flying) craft.

Over the first ten chapters of this book we discussed at length the historical and universal as well as esoteric and theological premise of dimensional beings ("deities") of superintelligence who throughout time have been depicted as guarding and sometimes passing through "gateways" of heaven, earth, great rivers, and sea. The phenomenon occurred/occurs on both a galactic and personal level. The myths surrounding the curiosity are both primeval and contemporary—from Sumerian deity descriptions to modern UFOnauts—and everything in between. The truly universal, redundant mythos surrounding these events provide the closest thing to empirical evidence for what one might call documentation of a genuine historical and possibly supernatural event. The manifestations began before the Tower of Babel (the gate of god) when almost instantly, populations around the world went from being hunter/gatherers to forming advanced civilizations mastering complicated mathematics, astronomy, science, and engineering techniques capable of building observatories and pyramids with astronomical qualities and similarity to one another . Among the most well-developed societies, sacred records of the "starting" phenomenon were kept by cargo cults and "holy men" who concerned themselves with "what" and "who" was seen, felt, and, according to Zechariah Sitchin, "served." These "record-keepers" also predicted a future time when the portals would reopen and the creator "gods" would return.

The question of whether beings of unknown origin truly interact with humans and at times somehow incarnate themselves through dimensional openings into three-dimensional (or four-dimensional if you add "time") reality is supported by archaeological, historical, and religious records, though not always standard anthropological or creation-models. Modern researchers nevertheless are increasingly convinced that something unexplainable did and perhaps still is happening in this regard. Vatican publications (as I predicted would happen on various radio programs and at *RaidersNewsNetwork.com* over the last two years) have recently released a series of publications dealing with the possibility of Extraterrestrial or multi-dimensional intelligence, hinting that a greater-than-not possibility of ET contact now exists. (Consolmagno)

At the 8th International Bioastronomy Conference in Reykjavik, Iceland, last year, more than 300 researchers and scientists discussed extraterrestrial intelligence with a similar conviction that the possibility of authentic contact with those who come through portals is now greater than ever. "It sounds almost metaphysical, but something is happening which we could not even have imagined," said Simon Conway Morris, Professor for Evolutionary Paleobiology at Cambridge University, summing up the nature of expectation following the week-long Bioastronomy Conference. Ulrich Dopatka who attended the conference for the Ancient Astronaut Society agreed, sensing among the scientists, astronomers, biologists, physicists, geneticists, biochemists, and paleontologists that "… a certain unrest or expectant tension…ran through the proceedings almost like a red thread, as if one were shortly before THE discovery…indications now speak in favor of a million, if not billion-fold expansion of evolutionary preconditions for ETIs [Extraterrestrial Intelligences] and, therefore, for a large number of existing, technological civilizations in our galaxy."

More recently, European astronomers announced the discovery of an Earth-like planet outside our solar system circling the red dwarf star, Gliese 581. Temporarily named 581 c, the planet has just the right temperatures and size to be habitable, a find described as a major step in the search for Extraterrestrial Intelligence.

Yet some believe there is no need to wait. "They" already are here and have been for some time. What "they" are up to is truly mysterious according to men like Missler and Eastman, who note in their critical work, *Alien Encounters*:

> The material we've examined to this point is indeed bizarre and in some cases unbelievable. And yet, we have seen that there is compelling evidence to believe that we have been visited, some would say 'invaded,' by aerially adept, shape-shifting, interdimensional beings. The origin and agenda of these beings is a topic of great dispute. Among researchers there are those who believe that the occupants of UFOs are benevolent, highly advanced beings who are here to share their knowledge and genetic material with mankind for the purpose of advancing our evolution. Others believe their behavior and message betray a sinister agenda. Some, like Jacques Vallée , believe that we may be on the threshold of a gigantic cosmic deception perpetrated by interdimensional beings whose purpose and agenda for mankind are unknown. (Missler and Eastman 236)

Others, like Stuart Goldman, think the motive and activity of these beings are not so unknown. Writing to John Weldon in a manuscript-letter which he called, "They're Here!," Goldman says:

> ...the unpleasant fact is, 50,000 people can not be lying. Something is here—probing people, inspecting them, and planting thoughts in their minds, manipulating their

bodies—treating them, in a sense, like so many cattle. Is it all simply a gigantic cosmic joke, or is there a more sinister plot at hand? Are we seeing the formation of a new and highly destructive cult, one whose view posits the elimination (the New Agers call it "spiritual cleansing") of people who are "unfit" to exist in the coming New World? Are there really demonic entities hovering about, searching for likely candidates whose brains and minds they can invade, filling them full of fairy tales and lies—fattening them for the kill? The answer is not easily forthcoming. But whichever scenario you may choose, the ominous statement of John Keel must—for all but the most hardened skeptics—ring in our ears. "The earth is not inhabited," says Keel. "It's infested." (Goldman 26)

If indeed the earth is "infested" by beings whose purposes can only now be guessed at, one thing seems increasingly clear: the dualistic worldview which Dr. John Mack discussed—the idea that the spiritual realm and material realm are separate parts of the same reality—may at last be known and sooner than many people are prepared for or can conceive. Parallels between "angels," "demons," and ET phenomena have been recognized by experts of different fields for some time. More and more question the "nuts-and-bolts" approach to defining UFOs (as in high tech mechanical space craft flying to earth from far galaxies) in favor of, for want of a better term, "spiritual conceptualization" of ET.

According to Dr. John Mack:

The alien beings that appear to come to us from the sky in strange spacecraft present a particularly confusing challenge.... For they seem to partake of properties

belonging to both the spirit and material worlds, bridg-
ing, as if effortlessly, the division between these realms
which have become increasingly sacred and unbreachable
since science and religion went their separate ways in the
seventeenth century. On the one hand these beings seem
able to be seen by the abductees, who feel their bodies
moved and find small lesions inflicted upon them. On
the other hand the beings seem to come, like interme-
diaries from God or the devil, from a nonembodied
source....My own impression is that we may be witness-
ing...an awkward joining of two species, engineered by
an intelligence we are unable to fathom....(John Mack
404-405)

In his book, *Witnessed,* Budd Hopkins agrees:

Everything I have learned in 20 years of research into
the UFO abduction phenomenon leads me to conclude
that the aliens' central purpose is not to teach us about
taking better care of the environment; instead, all of
the evidence points to their being here to carry out a
complex breeding experiment in which they seem to be
working to create a hybrid species, a mix of human and
alien characteristics. (Budd 378)

My wife and I fictionalized a worse-case scenario about this
in our book, *The Ahriman Gate*:

Tapping his finger against his palm as if to emphasize
the next point, Jones stressed, "And as far as how UFOs
would be used to deceive us, this comes down to an
argument of origins."

"Meaning what?"

"The ageless question—where did we come from? If people believe UFOnauts are advanced extraterrestrials scurrying about in spaceships, and that these same creatures visited the Earth in ancient days and tinkered with hominid DNA, that disturbs the Judeo-Christian doctrine concerning the age of the Earth and biblical creation. Satan would love people to believe we are nothing more than an alien zoology program. Of course," he said, rolling his eyes, "there's always Indy's Theory of UFOlogy."

"Indy's Theory? As in your own personal theory?"

"Mine and a few others."

Sheri smiled. "Tell us about this mysterious theory."

"I thought you'd never ask. According to the Bible, the End Times will be accompanied by fearful sights and great signs from heaven. The book of Second Thessalonians even says that, when the Antichrist is revealed, he will be accompanied by 'lying wonders.' Maybe these verses are talking about UFOs being used to introduce the Man of Sin. Wouldn't the world react to the sudden arrival of an intergalactic wise man with awe and wonder? The prophecies of Daniel seem to support this possibility."

"You're telling me the prophet Daniel talked about a Last Days invasion of UFOs?" Joe said, sounding incredulous.

"No, no. But he said the Antichrist will be a worshiper of Baal, and Baal was the lord of the sky. As Baalbamoth he was the lord of the aerial regions. As Baalzebub he was the lord of those that 'fly' or that flit about in the atmosphere. In the New Testament, Satan himself is referred to as the prince of the powers of the air. Therefore scriptures lead me to believe that the aerial phenomena you and I interpret as UFO activity *could* be part of a Last Days delusion—something to trick humanity into accepting the appearance of Antichrist."

Joe took a deep breath and exhaled slowly. *UFOs could introduce the Antichrist, huh?* He stared at the image. "So when it comes to these Annunaki, you believe we're talking about fallen angels?"

"In a nutshell, yes."

"And somehow this relates to our little image here."

"In ways I don't understand. To be honest, I'm amazed to see Sumerian written on it. If it's not a fake, I would…"

"I already told you it's real," Joe said, defensive of his father's claims.

Jones picked the image up and turned it over in his hand. "Don't be offended, Joe. I'm just a professor. We're paid to be cautious, even skeptical. So listen. I have a friend who runs an independent laboratory. He does all kinds of subcontract work for the state and federal government, mostly crime lab stuff, but also a little radiocarbon and metallurgy testing. If you'd let me borrow this thing for a couple days, I could have him run a series of tests on it to determine its age and material makeup. We could even do a photo analysis and database search to see if any comparable artifacts have been discovered or described in the past. This is the best way I know to provide an authoritative answer. With your permission, I'd like to take it to him right away." (Horn 74-75)

And later in our story…

Corsivino frowned. "We found our dream disintegrating. No matter how we tried, we couldn't replicate the Nibiruan Key's effect on the Enigma nor obtain the vortex described by the Dropa discs. To make matters worse, the project took an unexpected turn when advanced human DNA labeling was discovered in the Dropa. It illustrated genetic manipulation done by the Annunaki thousands of years before, including specific formulas for improving the human species."

Maybe Dr. Jones knew what he was talking about after all, Joe thought.

"The formulas called for introducing animal, and, in at least one case, alien DNA into human genome. Experts at the Pentagon quickly determined humanity had been the subject of unknown mutation experiments. They convened a black operations panel and concluded that regardless of what else the Dropa texts represented, the discovery provided a unique opportunity for human enhancement studies."

"So this is where you got involved, I take it," Dave said.

"Following the panel's above-top-secret report, genetic engineers like myself were given unprecedented resources, and the genome sciences were born."

"Sickening," Joe slipped.

Corsivino looked into his deep green eyes. "I understand. Not everybody was enthusiastic about our research back then, either. There were project scientists—those of religious persuasion—that came to believe the spacecraft and its contents were a remnant of forbidden technology, something cast down from heaven, perhaps a leftover of Lucifer's rebellion against God."

"Did they express these views?" Joe knew in the military that you usually keep your mouth shut, even when you disagree.

"A Jesuit named Malachi Malina did. He openly cautioned about dark forces he thought were trying to initiate Armageddon again, to unleash the Antichrist."

"What do you mean, trying again?"

"You know, another Hitler or Antiochus Epiphanes, except this time a very high-tech one. The Jesuit based his conclusions about the Nibiruan Key and its devilish connection on similarities between ancient history involving the Nibiruans, or Annunaki, and the genetic experiments growing out of our research."

This was really starting to sound like Jones now.

"He showed us where the Annunaki offered weapons technology to Israel's enemies in exchange for women. The antediluvian females became hosts to genetic experiments, resulting in a breed of giants called Nephilim."

"Like Goliath," Dave said.

"According to Malina, yes. Goliath was one of an army of giants, created to destroy God's people and to take over the world. God thwarted the original plan by eliminating the ancient Nephilim."

"And that was that." Dave said.

"I wish it were that simple. Malina believed history was repeating itself—that the disc recovered from Sedona was a Trojan horse—something to trick world governments into joining forces with Satan in preparation of Armageddon. Malina even speculated that the alien bodies we had recovered were demonic concoctions."

"Sounds like something a friend told me recently," Joe said to Corsivino.

"What's that?"

"Dr. Jones, a friend of the family, he believes aliens and demons are one and the same."

"Father Malina was convinced of it, and he claimed it was illustrated in history books from civilizations around the world."

"History books? You mean mythology, don't you?" Dave corrected.

"Both. I remember Malina discussing the Greek Titans, how their legend began with so-called gods mating with earth women. He compared that story to Genesis where the Sons of God took women for wives and their offspring became mighty men of old. He also showed us how the word Titan equals 666 in Greek and means 'gray, whitish, or chalky gray,' fitting the skin coloration of the bodies recovered at Sedona. He certainly felt we were opening the gates to an ancient perdition by tinkering with this alien technology."

"So...he's the one that convinced you to quit?" Joe asked, referring to Malina.

"What started me thinking we scientists had been duped was a meeting between Major General William H. Layton, the secretary of defense, and Montero's top genetic researchers."

Joe recognized the Major General's name. He had heard him speak while he was stationed in Hawaii. He was definitely a command presence, not somebody to second-guess.

"He told us that Special Agent Apol Leon—a military expert of some kind—would be in charge of genetic research in our department from there on out. We were becoming an All Black operation. No information concerning our undertaking was to be divulged to any military or government departments outside our own. This was now a top-level national security issue. Of course we voiced our allegiance and reaffirmed our oaths, but the ethics of our work certainly changed after Apol Leon, and Hell, came to Montero."

It suddenly dawned on Joe that Corsivino was talking about the man on his answering machine at home. He froze and listened carefully.

"Mr. Leon was on special assignment from Wright-Patterson Airforce Base where the alien bodies were kept. After formal introduction of him, General Layton disclosed top secret information related to an advanced race of humanoids, which supposedly visited Earth some ten thousand years ago."

"What proof did they offer of that allegation?" Dave said smartly.

"What proof did they need to offer? We had the alien bodies and their ship."

Dave opened his hands, palms up. "I mean that Earth was visited ten thousand years ago?"

"According to General Layton, the aliens left evidence of their visit everywhere—the pyramids, Nazca Lines, even an ancient city on Mars where excavations were underway by joint US-Soviet stealth expeditions. We were told in no uncertain terms that these aliens were our creators. Homo sapiens was the product of their genetic handiwork on apes."

Joe stared across the room at Dave's computers again. He was familiar with many US political and military figures. This was astounding information and probably confirmed Dave's worst conspiracy fears. He returned his sights to Corsivino and said, "General Layton actually said that?"

"Not only that. We were told of a second, more aggressive breed of creature called Anakim. The aliens made them to rule over the newly created people. Each Anakim had the strength of ten men. They were ruthless, but outnumbered by the humans. Eventually they were killed by hordes of men after the aliens, who were also known as 'flying geniuses,' departed for outer space. According to General Layton, the death of the Anakim was recorded in the mythos of every ancient culture, including the Bible, where the Hebrews called them Nephilim."

"But why would a Major General get involved with all this mythology?"

"A newly deciphered portion of the Dropa had caught his attention. It provided the genetic formula for recreating the Anakim-Nephilim. Needless to say, the military was profoundly interested in it. This represented the ultimate soldier, a perfect killing machine, and Apol Leon was at Montero to introduce our researchers to the technology we would use to manufacture them— the cutting-edge science of transgenics."

Joe realized he was clenching his fists again. His head was tilted down, his eyes fixed on Corsivino. He needed to calm down, think about his plan, glean as much information as he could from this man before making his move. He bit his lip and said, "So, Apol Leon came to teach you about transgenics, huh, the technology you would use to re-create the Nephilim. What does that actually mean?"

"Simply stated, transgenics is the science of altering

the genetic structure of one species by introducing the DNA of a different species into its genome. Under Apol's watchful eye, transgenics at Montero developed in the form of male human embryos having their molecular biology altered through inserting animal and alien DNA into their genome."

"Just where does one get alien DNA? I assume you don't run to the corner market for it."

Corsivino grinned. "From the specimens we recovered at Sedona. Those strands produced the most fascinating and horrific results."

Dave shook his head. "I hate to think what *that* means."

"Mutated embryos aggressive inside their mother's wombs, highly intelligent, brutish creatures after birth, babies with phenomenal growth rates, an unequivocal thirst to rule, conquer, and dominate."

"You must have been so proud," Joe smirked again. *Remember! Diplomacy!*

"Actually, we were flabbergasted. At six months of age the real problems developed. The chimera—or *Nephilim* as Apol insisted we call them—became uncontrollable. Due to their size and physical strength, special cages had to be designed to hold them. A few months after that we found it necessary to implant control chips directly into their brains."

"Evidently those chips were not foolproof at supervising your babies."

"What? Why do you say that?"

"Because at least one of them escaped," Joe said. He took a moment to fill Corsivino and Dave in on the recovery near Montero. He described the appearance of the carcass, the arm that was now in Dr. Jones's possession, and the wire inside the beast's head. He speculated that Jones was having the specimen tested at Nathan Reel's laboratory.

Corsivino's reaction was one of astonishment. "That's what he had in the blanket at the hillside? This arm?"

"Affirmative."

"Well, when and if that arm's DNA is analyzed, a fifth and sixth nucleotide will be discovered. It's unlike anything ever seen in animal or human DNA before. It could really open a can of worms."

Good. "And the wire in the giant's head? That was one of your control devices?"

"It's called AngelStar. It too was a product of reverse engineering, actually designed for human implantation. The aggressive nature of the Nephilim forced us to interface the neural chip with the beast's brains, in order to control them. From what I remember it caused the creatures to become lethargic when set at one hundred sixteen megahertz."

Dave, sounding like his contemptible old self again, said, "But did it satisfy naysayers?"

"What do you mean, naysayers?"

"The scientists that were uncomfortable with the project…the Malina guy and the others who thought this might be an Antichrist thing. Were they willing to go along with the research once they saw the ape-men could be controlled?"

Corsivino looked confused by the question and said, "The fact that we learned to control the beasts was a separate issue to Malina and his colleagues. Questions about the ethics of our research grew regardless, even among the nonreligious types. Eventually, I found myself among them."

Joe raised an eyebrow. "I thought you said you were a project leader?"

"I was, but you must understand, Joe, even though I knew I was breaking my own values, there was something alluring about our work. It was as if a beautiful Siren stood somewhere in the distance, bidding us to come to her. It drew us back day after day with promises of discovery and immortality. Indeed, we believed our work would immortalize us in more ways than one."

"But you were finally convinced otherwise?"

"It all came to a head one day during a casual conversation with Malachi Malina. He'd been removed from the research program at Montero a week before. The official reasoning was ambiguous, but we all knew Malachi was terminated as a result of his challenging the ethics of Montero's research. In the days following his departure, Malachi contacted several team members, including myself. He couldn't speak publicly, so he chose to address his former co-workers privately, to challenge our moral apathy. In my case, he specifically wondered why as a professing Christian I was not concerned with my role at Montero, why I couldn't see it as an affront to the divine order."

Joe was incredulous. "You're a Christian?"

"Is that so hard to believe?"

"With the work you were involved in? Yes, as a matter of fact."

"Then you and Father Malina would have agreed. He came right out and asked me. 'Andrew,' he said, 'the Bible tells us that God commands humans, animals, and plants to reproduce after their own kind. If God requires species integrity, how do you reconcile what you are doing? Your research at Montero not only violates Scripture, but could open a Pandora's box to a molecular biological nightmare.'"

"He was right," Joe said, not that he understood the science.

"I know, in many ways, I see that now. By introducing animal and alien DNA into human genome, we were breaching the species barrier and producing unclassified mutations beyond imagination."

Joe couldn't help himself. Even though he wanted to play this guy, he scoffed, "Yet you remained. I sure hope the pay was good."

"Actually, I left the program not long after Malina did."

"I remember that," Dave said, raising his finger. "It was big news."

Joe was more interested in what motivated him. "Was it a conflict of conscience, or were you just protecting your butt somehow?"

"I'd say a mixture of both, although my conscience drives me these days, believe it or not."

"That's not an answer."

"Okay, in particular, the problem for me was this: The molecular biologists at Montero classified the functions of the alien genes supplied by Apol Leon. Yet none of them knew how the gene's coding would react from the alien species to human. There were strong possibilities that interspecies differences would measurably effect the gene's protein interactions, thus modifying the human hereditary traits in the mutations. That represented a potential catastrophe beyond measure."

Joe hoped he would rephrase the comment so he could understand the important point.

As if reading his mind, Corsivino said, "Let me put it a different way. Since interbreeding between humans and Nephilim was now theoretically possible, it was reasonable to believe the mutated DNA would get out of the bottle someday. When that happened, alien and animal characteristics would be introduced to our own species, altering the human genetic code and eventually eliminating humanity as we know it. Malachi Malina believed this was not only possible, but also perhaps the whole idea. That was something I could not be part of."

Joe was contemplative, then finally said, "Sounds like a Dr. Jones theory."

"Meaning?"

"Something the professor told me about God having to destroy the human race during Noah's flood because giants had interbred with humans. According to Jones, by the time Noah and his children came along, they were the only ones left with DNA not corrupted by intermarriage with Nephilim and their offspring. In order to preserve the human species, God had to eliminate everybody but Noah and his family."

"Jones is a smart man," Corsivino said. "What would you say if I told you a similar plan is unfolding as we speak, right beneath the world's nose?"

"I'd hope you were kidding. A plan to annihilate mankind by interbreeding humans with Nephilim? Why would anybody want to do that?"

"They are deceived. The government and military are deceived. They believe their research is leading to a super army that will police a New World Order—a better world system. Those of us in Operation Gadfly think differently. We believe Montero's work is part of a larger scheme to force Armageddon and to enslave mankind."

Dave raised his hand again. "Operation Gadfly?"

"It's a consortium of scientists dedicated to the destruction of Montero, its research and researchers, and similar factories around the world."

"You mean there's more than one factory!?"

"Oh yes. Nine others in the Alliance of Nations. Ten in total." (Horn 133-145)

Chapter 12

PERSUASION
OF THE ANTICHRIST

As noted earlier, many UFO investigators have documented redundant comparisons between some conditions of "alien" activity and "demonism" (malevolence). This aspect of UFO phenomenon is almost inevitably tied to generational "abduction" scenarios and often includes occult practices and belief. Pardon the following repetitive commentary as I believe it is important to establish in the mind of the reader certain qualified conclusions from experts in various fields of Ufology.

In 1969, Lynn E. Catoe was senior bibliographer of UFO research, conducted by the Library of Congress for the Air Force Office of Scientific Research Project Order 67-0002 and 68-0003. After two-years and thousands of documents, she concluded that, "A large part of the available UFO literature... deals with subjects like mental telepathy, automatic writing and invisible entities...poltergeist manifestations and 'possession.' Many...UFO reports...recount alleged incidents that are strikingly similar to demonic possession and psychic phenomena" (Wikipedia, Paranormal and occult hypotheses about UFOs).

Professor Elizabeth L. Hillstrom in her book *Testing the Spirits* agrees that a growing number of academics have also concluded that UFOnauts are synonymous with historical demonism. "Vallée's explanation of UFOs is the most striking," she says:

> because of its parallels with demonic activity. UFO investigators have noticed these similarities. Vallée himself, drawing from extra biblical literature on demonic activities, establishes a number of parallels between UFOnauts and demons....Pierre Guerin, a UFO researcher and a scientist associated with the French National Council for Scientific Research, is not so cautious: "The modern UFOnauts and the demons of past days are probably identical." Veteran researcher John Keel, who wrote *UFOs: Operation Trojan Horse* and other books on the subject, comes to the same conclusion: "The UFO manifestations seem to be, by and large, merely minor variations of the age-old demonological phenomenon." (Hillstrom 207-208)

Whitley Strieber, author of *Communion* and other books on the subject, says in *Transformation*:

> I felt an absolutely indescribable sense of menace. It was hell on earth to be there, and yet I couldn't move, couldn't cry out, couldn't get away...Whatever was there seemed so monstrously ugly, so filthy and dark and sinister. Of course they were demons. They had to be. And they were here and I couldn't get away. (Strieber 190)

Earlier he recounts:

There are worse things than death, I suspected. And I was beginning to get the distinct impression that one of them had taken an interest in me. So far the word demon had never been spoken among the scientists and doctors who were working with me. And why should it have been? We were beyond such things. We were a group of atheists and agnostics, far too sophisticated to be concerned with such archaic ideas as demons and angels. (Strieber 36)

While some Ufologists see the reoccurring malevolent "visitation" or abduction theme as genuinely demonic (that is, fallen angels or disembodied warrior spirits—enemies of God and humanity—seeking to corrupt the human race and/or to recreate Homo sapiens in their image), other Ufologists see just the opposite, claiming that the writers of the Bible simply interpreted the unknown phenomena in the same way the rest of us might have—the best way we could and within our own particular worldviews.

Yet, do ancient records including the Genesis 6 account support the theory that alien creatures traveled from distant planets or other dimensions in UFOs, performed reproductive experiments on women, and were afterward honored in the images and folklore of the gods of mythology? Or is the story in Genesis and elsewhere a record of fallen angels acting in accord with Satan? What, if anything, would this tell us about the origin of the gods and the current interstellar phenomena? Are we experiencing an ongoing invasion of earth by intergalactic scientists or is "Satan" busy advancing the most sophisticated con in history?

Some believe the latter is the case and that in the end times "...fearful sights and great signs...from heaven" (Lk 21.11) will see Satan contriving an "alien invasion" to explain: 1) those taken in a "rapture" (New Agers would call this "the cleansing"); or 2) the introduction of Antichrist.

Second Thess. 2.8-12 says:

And then shall that Wicked [one] be revealed...whose coming is after the working of Satan with all power and signs and lying wonders . . . And for this cause God shall send them strong delusion, that they should believe a lie: That they all might be damned who believed not the truth, but had pleasure in unrighteousness.

The idea is that when the Antichrist is revealed, he will be accompanied by "lying wonders"—i.e., UFOs being used to introduce the Man of Sin.

Of course the world would react to the sudden arrival of an intergalactic super man with awe and wonder, and some cannot help but connect this fact with the prophet Daniel's discussion of an Antichrist who will worship Baal—the lord of the sky (Baalbamoth was the lord of the aerial regions and Baalzebub was the lord of those that "fly" or that flit about in the atmosphere). In the New Testament, Satan is referred to as being the prince of the powers of the air, scriptures that lead some to believe the aerial phenomena interpreted as UFO activity could be part of a Last Days delusion—something to trick humanity into accepting the appearance of an Antichrist. If suddenly hundreds of "space craft" visibly arrived in our atmosphere, they say, piloted by beings who appeared to be advanced humanoids, these beings could arguably claim to have removed "believers" into a high-tech "rapture" and/or simultaneously present their leader

(Antichrist?) as the awaited messiah (Quetzalcoatl? Dionysus?). Under this scenario, these beings might also point to ancient megaliths, pyramids, and the gods of mythology as proof of an ancient visitation of planet earth by them as the Elohim.

The late Pulitzer Prize-winning author Carl Sagan was, until his death, working on a screenplay about the ramifications of just such a savior who appears in the coming millennium.

In the new *Superman Returns* movie from Warner Brothers, director Bryan Singer plays off the apocalyptic end-of-the-world-scenario accompanied by a "savior" who appears from the sky in the nick of time to rescue humanity from annihilation. The trailer for *Superman Returns* repeats the strong messiah-symbolism seen in recent films *The Matrix* and *Star Wars*. Superman's celestial (heavenly) father says:

> …They can be a great people, Kal-El, if they wish to be. They only lack the light to show the way. For this reason above all—all their capacity for good—I have sent them you, my only son.

BEWARE THE COMING SUPERMAN-SAVIOR?

Whatever has been going on for centuries that defines the UFO/Alien phenomenon is ultimately connected to the history of angels, demons, fairies, incubi, succubi, and the gods of mythology. Again we note Jacques Vallée drawing strong similarity between occupants of UFOs and supernatural entities.

> I had shown in Passport to Magonia that contact with ufonauts was only a modern extension of the age-old tradition of contact with nonhuman consciousness in the form of angels, demons, elves, and sylphs. (Vallée 159)

John Keel echoes this scholarship in *Operation Trojan Horse*, where he states:

> Demonology is not just another crackpot-ology. It is the ancient and scholarly study of the monsters and demons who have seemingly coexisted with man throughout history.... . The manifestations and occurrences described in this imposing literature are similar, if not entirely identical, to the UFO phenomenon itself. Victims of demonomania (possession) suffer the very same medical and emotional symptoms as the UFO contactees.... The Devil and his demons can, according to the literature, manifest themselves in almost any form and can physically imitate anything from angels to horrifying monsters with glowing eyes. Strange objects and entities materialize and dematerialize in these stories, just as the UFOs and their splendid occupants appear and disappear, walk through walls, and perform other supernatural feats. (Keel 192)

Later in *Operation Trojan Horse*, Keel spoke of the intangible nature of the aliens and their craft as "transmogrifications tailoring themselves to our ability to understand" (Keel 266). Dr. John Mack not only made the same conclusion—that the UFOnauts illustrate behavior resembling historical demons—but that the intangible nature of such is illustrated in how ETs traverse dimensional gateways, portals, and stargates, such as we have focused on in this study.

In *Abduction*, Mack writes:

> Quite a few abductees have spoken to me of their sense that at least some of their experiences are not occur-

ring within the physical space-time dimensions of the universe as we comprehend it. They speak of aliens breaking through from another dimension, through a "slit" or "crack" in some sort of barrier [gateway, portal], entering our world from "beyond the veil." Abductees, some of whom have little education to prepare them to explain about such abstractions or odd dislocations, will speak of the collapse of space-time that occurs during their experiences. They experience the aliens, indeed their abductions themselves, as happening in another reality, although one that is as powerfully actual to them as—or more so than—the familiar physical world. (Mack 402)

In several parts of our newest book—the appropriately named *The Ahriman Gate*—we fictionalize the nature of these "alien" space-time portals, such as here:

Desperation more than courage pulled Joe like potent gravity into the darkness. Even as the lights came on and his eyes adjusted to the details, the trace glow of the vanishing phantoms—like psychic shadows searching for ways to rush through spectral dimensions—lingered before him. The pungent smell of decaying flesh gripped the air as he turned the M-249 along the walls, fingering the trigger, fearful that the jittering in his belly might give way to unrestrained machine gun spray. Finally, satisfied that the *things* were gone, he lowered the weapon and moved toward Sheri...

As Sheri gazed silently upward, Phobos shifted his attention back to the corner of the room. The grays had dematerialized there like ectoplasm through a fantastic-spinning void. He wasn't sure what he would have done even if he had caught the fiends, but the simple act of their fleeing had invigorated his nerve. He clutched the crucifix in his pocket and reminded himself to be careful; overconfidence against such beings could be fatal, even if he did understand spiritual warfare as taught by Father Malina. (Horn 288-289)

So exactly what are the experts saying? Given that most UFO researchers—religious and secular—agree on this important point—that often the beings who come through portals (demons or ET) are one and the same—the question is begged, "What are the ETs up to?"

The answer seems to revolve around alleged abduction and hybrid-breeding. Dr. Mack, Vallée, Keel, and other experts have in their own ways rehearsed the age old story of those who "from heaven to earth came" and conducted genetic alteration on humans, finally departing into space, leaving behind promises of a future return.

The familiar Genesis story of Watchers cohabiting with women parallels the modern "abduction" reports in that the "…sons of God…took them wives of all which they chose" (Gen. 6.2). The implication here is that, as in alien abduction, this was not by mutual agreement or harmony of wills but that these women were taken ("took") forcibly at the sole discretion of the powerful beings. As a result of the abduction-marriages, hybrids were born called "Nephilim."

Eric von Däniken and Zecharia Sitchin go so far as to use this same portion of the Bible—Genesis 6—as proof that the "sons of God" (Annunaki of Sumeria) were the extraterrestrials of their literature who performed genetic modification on Homo sapiens.

SO WHERE IS ALL OF THIS LEADING?

Given the abundant and universal prophecies that the "end times" will witness what we have been calling a "reopening of the gates of heaven" and the descending of a "savior," it is important to note that from the Middle Ages forward, many church leaders have believed that the Antichrist would ultimately represent the return of the Nephilim—the union of a demon and a human.

St. Augustine writes of such demoniality in the *City of God* (Augustine) and in the *De Daemonialitate, et Incubis, et Succubi,* Fr. Ludovicus Maria Sinistrari de Ameno (1622-1701) qualifies the connection between hybridization of demons and humans:

> To theologians and philosophers, it is a fact, that from the copulation of humans (man or woman) with the demon, human beings are sometimes born. It is by this process that Antichrist must be born, according to a number of doctors…the children generated in this manner by the incubi are tall, very strong, very daring, very magnificent and very wicked…(Fr. Ludovicus 127-129)

Phobos clarifies this for Joe in our novel, *The Ahriman Gate*.

> Joe raised the special container with a heavy sigh. "So, if Apollyon is somehow embodied in Apol, we could actually be carrying the embryo of the *Antichrist* here?"
>
> "That's correct. According to the Bible, the Antichrist will be 'the son of perdition,' the male progeny of the Greek *apoleia*, or Apollyon. The implication couldn't be clearer—the Man of Sin will be the physical offspring of the destroyer demon, a transgenic of the highest order."
> (Horn 326-327)

And elsewhere:

He'd never run short of such material. A typical woman supplied thousands of eggs, and the process for multiplication, unlike at other government funded cloning labs, had been solved at Montero thanks to the Dropa, which explained the process of cell division in humans and primates using a combination of egg fertilization to jump-start spindle formation. After that, it was a simple process of replacing the human DNA with Apol's. As the alien cells divided into two cells, then four, Apol would manually separate the cells and allow the replication process to start again. By dividing cells in this way, he had created as many as sixteen single-cell embryos at a time. All but one were typically frozen, while the remaining embryo stayed in the petri dish, dividing, specializing: transforming into Homo nephilim.

Yet unlike regular Nephilim code, which had been highly successful, every embryo made of Apol's special DNA had degenerated into worthless cell matter before developing far enough to be implanted, or died shortly thereafter.

Yet any day now, he told himself, he would triumph. His son, the son of perdition, would inevitably be conceived. It had to. The Enigma was about to open, and the Master would step through it. *He* would expect a body, a host for his transmigration; the biblical seed of Satan depended on it. (Horn 157-158)

If the Antichrist is in fact at length the physical offspring of a demon, not only will he be the exact opposite of Jesus (son of God) but the forerunner of the return of the Nephilim. This fact could be contemporary given that Jesus said the end times would be as the days of Noah, and the prophet Isaiah (chapters 13 and 14) also tied the return of the Nephilim to the destruction of the city of Babylon in the end of days (look to current war activities in Iraq).

In Isaiah 13.1-3, 9, 19-22 (Septuagint Version) the prophet says:

> The vision which Esaias son of Amos saw against Babylon. Lift up a standard on the mountain of the plain, exalt the voice to them, beckon with the hand, open the gates, ye ruler. I give command and I bring them: giants are coming to fulfill my wrath, rejoicing at the same time and insulting.... For behold! the day of the Lord is coming which cannot be escaped, a day of wrath and anger, to make the world desolate....And Babylon... shall be as when God overthrew Sodoma and Gomorrah....It shall never be inhabited...and monsters shall rest there, and devils shall dance there and satyrs shall dwell there....(Septuagint)

One can only speculate if something more than is casually perceived was meant when Isaiah said, "...*open the gates, ye ruler...*" Who was this *ruler*? And are these the *gates* to the city, or something more unusual? Don't be quick to bypass this question, as the "Mighty ones" of the King James and other Bible versions is *Gibborim*—the same Hebrew term used elsewhere in ancient literature to describe the Nephilim which are correctly translated here in the Greek as "giants." The fantastic conclusion from this is that Isaiah may literally be telling us that when Babylon is invaded and destroyed in the last days, God will command (unleash from their prisons? Command the "ruler" to open their gate?) giant Nephilim to come forth as agents of destruction. This astonishing prophecy is further amplified by the invasion of US forces and the ongoing occupation of the ancient city of Babylon, where thousands of troops admittedly filled their sandbags with archaeological material (Charles), causing some to wonder if cuneiform tablets with information about lost exotic technology were recovered or, even more alarming, tablets with ancient diagrams leading to pure-blooded Nephilim buried beneath the sands in underground caves. Just imagine the interest agencies like DARPA would have in studying (cloning?) this ancient DNA. Could something of this nature be the method by which Isaiah's prophecy is fulfilled? Could man in his arrogance revive ancient DNA, revitalizing or blending it with other living organisms is a way similar to what the Watchers did in making the first Nephilim? Is this why the Rephaim (dead Nephilim) are viewed as squirming beneath the earth, waiting for resurrection? Is this why Isaiah predicted monsters, satyrs and devils accompanying the giants in Babylon and why other Apocryphal Books such as 2 Esdras 5:8 confirm the birth of "monsters" in the last days?

The Defense Advanced Research Projects Agency (DARPA) has invested heavily in projects such as the "Extended Performance Warfighter" project, which among other things includes genetic alteration of future soldiers (Floyd). The idea of genetically modifying humans is exactly what the Watchers did, and one notes with regard to the biblical "mighty ones" and their connection with Babylon, that when "…Cush begat Nimrod: he began to be a *mighty one* in the earth….And the beginning of his kingdom was *Babel*…" [emphasis added] (Gen 10.8-10). The relationship between Babylon (the gate of god), genetic modification, and the first giants, as well as the prophesied destruction of Babylon in the end times by returning giants, is stunning in light of recent advances in biotechnology coupled with the US invasion of Babylon. It is starting to look as if world history is playing out according to script.

Lastly, when I speculated recently in the so-called "Famous Q-Files Bedtime Story" that perhaps the US had invaded Iraq for reasons other than what has been admitted thus far, people were quick to contact me regarding the inference to Babylonian stargates. Given that the Book of Enoch (recognized in the New Testament in such places as Jude 6 and 2 Peter 2.4) says that the Watchers first descended to earth on Mount Hermon during the days of Jared, and considering David Flynn's incredible research into Mount Hermon and the year 2012 earlier in this book, and lastly that some mid-tribulation "rapture" believers count backwards seven years from 2012 to the current hour, some believe we may have entered Daniel's seventieth week.

Whatever the case may be, something was in Babylon in olden days. According to Bible prophecy, it will be again... *already is?!?*

Alea iacta est—"The die has been cast."
—Caesar

Chapter 13

ANOTHER TOWER
OF BABEL

n the last chapter we noted Isaiah marking the end of time by destruction of Babylon (Iraq) and the return of terrible giants (Nephilim) when God commands a "ruler" to "open the gates," releasing giants to fulfill His wrath. What God did in Egypt when "He cast upon them the fierceness of His anger…by sending *evil angels* among them" [emphasis added] (Ps. 78.49), he will do again. Yet, Isaiah's prophecy is additionally fascinating given that Nimrod, the designer of the Tower of Babel—the "gate of god"—was himself a Nephilim [Gibborim] (see 1 Chron. 1.10).

In *Cydonia: The Secret Chronicles of Mars*, David E. Flynn takes this a step further, connecting Nimrod's construction of the Tower of Babel to the rebel planet Mars.

> Nimrod…a giant of the race of Nephilim…authored the plan for the tower…[and was] associated in myth with Nergal, the Babylonian god of Mars… *The Tower of Babel was a tower to Mars.* [emphasis added] (Flynn 105)

Earlier in his astonishing book, Flynn points out:

Symbolism used by the mystery schools illuminated the writings of Italian poet Dante, who [also] wrote of the connections between the Tower of Babel, Giants and Mars. Intriguingly, Dante identified Mars with Satan. Paradiso Canto IX:127-142:

> Florence, the city founded by Mars, that Satan who first turned his back on his Maker, and from whose envy such great grief has come, coins and spreads that accursed lily flower, that has sent the sheep and lambs astray, since it has made a wolf of the shepherd.
>
> The ancient Cabiri (Gibborim) who built Cyclopean walls and megalithic fortresses took many forms, but they all originated from the same place. They came down from heaven to the earth. According to ancient Sumerian myth, when Nergal the god of Mars was ejected from heaven he descended with...demons...(Flynn 105)

Thus, not only was Nimrod a Nephilim, not only did he design the Tower of Babel ("gate of god"), not only was he associated with Mars and built the tower of Babel to the rebel prison planet, but he, like other giants, was daimonic (demonic) in origin. The significance of this cannot be overlooked. Babel was a *Nephilim gateway,* and it is prophesied to be the future location from which "gates" open and "giants" return.

ANCIENT ADVANCED SCIENCE
AND DID GOD MEAN WHAT HE SAID?

Genesis 11 tells the story of the tower of Babel. The builders wanted to create a structure "... whose top may reach unto heaven [Hebrew *shaw-mah'-yim*]" (Gen. 11.4). When the Lord came down and saw what was happening, he said, "...nothing will be restrained from them, which they have imagined to do" (Gen. 11.6).

This comment seems curious if the meaning here is only that the tower would reach into the "sky." Structures had been built around the world since the dawn of time extending significantly upward. Yet, as far as I know, none of them created a response from God, saying, "...nothing will be restrained from them, which they have imagined to do." Josephus points out that the Tower of Babel was being made waterproof and that this was an act of rebellion against God, defying him for sending the Flood and preparing for survival of future acts of punishment should they come. Yet, what if something else is meant here? Something that fits "which they have imagined to do" more perfectly with scripture and history? Something that points to the physicality of Heaven—as in the dwelling place of angels—and/or the peripheral nearness of the Ahriman Gate?

Keep in mind that, like the Bible often has, I am drawing finite abstractions for human comprehension with this question: How close to the surface of the earth is the dwelling place of angels? Of demons? Of God? I ask this because human nature tends to place the physical (for want of a better term) location of these domains far out into space. Yet, what if the "heavens" are so close as to have been reached upon tall mountains? The

Nephilim had intimate knowledge of the original earth before the heavens were closed-up and before God no longer walked with man in the cool of the evening. Did the Nephilim—as offspring of fallen angels—know something about the periphery of Kosmos and/or the throne room of God that we do not? Did they know that in some way these locations are just above our heads? Is this why Holy people throughout time have felt driven subconsciously to ascend mountains in search of God? Is this why scriptural and extra-biblical literature universally depict metaphors of heaven attained upon elevated platforms—Jacob's ladder, Quetzalcoatl's ladder, the gods upon the Mount of Olympus, the feet of the returning Christ upon the Mount of Olives, Moses receiving the Law from God upon Sinai, and the Watchers descending upon Mount Hermon? Is this why Nimrod, a Nephilim, built the tower of Babel whose top would reach into heaven?

Scientist Stan Deyo has done analysis of a Tower of Babel Stele with speculation about whether the original Tower of Babel was actually designed to facilitate reaching "the heavens" as indicated in the comments above. Was it a building whose top was high enough to allow higher-dimensional beings to descend slowly while discharging voltage directly into the lower energy density universe? Deyo notes the uppermost portion of the stele may show a "bright" or burning circular area, while the edges of the tower layers themselves are smooth like a high voltage insulator, as if for dissipating electricity. Stan emphasizes the analysis is inconclusive at this time, but it is interesting, given that beings who descended from heaven were typically accompanied by fire or lightning (electrical discharge?), while beings that ASCEND from lower energy densities (regions) tend to cool the atmosphere, such as in the classic "ghost" entering a room. Ancient artwork that may support this theory is widespread throughout ancient times including depictions of gods accompanied by fire.

We actually used this hypothesis above—a stargate above a pyramid or a high tower—for the design of the cover of this book. One also cannot help wonder if freemasons involved in the design of US currency did not know something of the meaning of gods descending on towers when they placed a brilliant all-seeing eye above the pyramid on the back of the dollar bill or when similar initiates of mystery religion designed the Pentagon's data mining service—the Information Awareness Office. And did you ever wonder why the top stone of the Great Pyramid is not in place? Kind of makes you wonder if NASA and DARPA's work on developing a tower into space made from carbon nanotubes, and a space elevator, is reverse engineering of technology recovered from Iraq or something needed for the return of the Sumerian gods!?

On the one hand the idea that "heaven" is just above our heads could bring comfort, to conceptualize God and his angels in such close proximity. On the other hand this notion brings significance to the prophecies of Isaiah regarding earthly Babelgates opening at the end of time during a period of war in Iraq when, according to the prophet, the earth will be invaded by destructive, emerging Nephilim.

WHEN DANIEL FOUGHT THE GATEKEEPER

In the tenth chapter of Daniel the story unfolds of the prophet praying for twenty-one days before the angel Gabriel appeared to say, "...from the first day thou didst set thine heart to understand, and to chasten thyself before thy God, they words were heard, and I am come for thy words" (Dan. 10.12).

Why did it take Gabriel twenty-one days to arrive? Because a powerful Persian demon had opposed him, and not until Michael, the archangel, came to help was Gabriel free to continue his journey.

In Persian theology this opposing spirit would have been identified as Ahriman. In the Book of Daniel he is simply called "the prince of the kingdom of Persia" (Iraq/Iran). He was the Babel gatekeeper, as fictionalized in our book—*The Ahriman Gate.*

God also revealed to Daniel (Chapter 7) other types of earthly "kingdom" influences: the Babylonian, the Medo-Persian, the Greek, and the Roman, each of which was a mere human agency under the control of supernatural powers. The principality of the Medo-Persian kingdom was depicted as a warmongering spirit seeking to dominate through military aggression, while its predecessor Babylonia was characterized by "forces" pretending to the throne of God.

Throughout the Bible, spiritual Babylon is equivalent to the world system that is at enmity with God. Babylon began at the Tower of Babel, where at the macro level Satan's strategy to incarnate a one-world system was first attempted. It now appears that it will end there, as the world hurdles toward a final climactic encounter with giants...and their "ruler."

FORERUNNER OF THE GIANTS?

Preceding Daniel's visit by Gabriel, a dream from Nebuchadnezzar, King of Babylon, gave Daniel insight concerning these kingdoms and the final "revived" empire that will ultimately provide the grand entry for the mother (*or should we say father?!*) of all Nephilim—the Antichrist of End Times prophecy. Daniel's prediction is amazing in light of the extraordinary references made in chapter 2:

And whereas thou sawest iron mixed with miry clay, they shall mingle themselves with the seed of men: but they shall not cleave one to another, even as iron is not mixed with clay. (Dan. 2.43)

The personal pronoun, *they* "shall mingle themselves with the seed of men..." causes Missler and Eastman in their book *Alien Encounters* to ask appropriately:

Just what (or who) are "mingling with the seed of men?" Who are these Non-seed? It staggers the mind to contemplate the potential significance of Daniel's passage and its implications for the future global governance. (Missler and Eastman 275)

When Daniel's prophecy is coupled with Genesis 3, an incredible tenet emerges—that *Satan has <u>seed</u>, and <u>it</u> is at enmity with Christ!*

And I will put enmity between thee and the woman, and between thy seed and her seed; it shall bruise thy head, and thou shalt bruise his heel. (Gen. 3.15)

The word translated here as "seed" is the Hebrew word *zera,* which means "offspring, descendants, children."

Is Satan's "posterity" lurking behind gates, waiting for a final opportunity to mingle themselves with human DNA, as in days of old? Is this the method by which the Nephilim will return? Is this, as noted earlier in this book concerning demoniality, the method by which Antichrist himself will be incarnated? If Genesis 6 is truly an account of rebel angels leaving their assigned habitation and cohabiting with human females—out of which union mutant life forms were born—is it reasonable to assume that Satan, as a fallen angel, already has, or will be allowed ability to copulate with a woman?

In *The Ahriman Gate* my wife and I answer:

> That's correct. According to the Bible, the Antichrist will be "the son of perdition," the male progeny of the Greek *apoleia*, or Apollyon. The implication couldn't be clearer—the Man of Sin will be the physical offspring of the destroyer demon, a transgenic of the highest order. (Horn 327)

THE FATHER OF NEPHILIM
AND THE SON OF PERDITION

Some believe that in the very near future a man of superior intelligence, wit, charm, and diplomacy will descend from the clouds or otherwise emerge on the world scene as a savior. He will seemingly possess a transcendent wisdom that enables him to solve problems and offer solutions to many of today's most perplexing issues. His popularity will be widespread, and his fans will include young and old, religious and non-religious, male and female. Talk show hosts will interview his colleagues, news anchors will cover his movements, scholars will applaud his uncanny ability at resolving what has escaped the rest of us, and the poor will bow down at his table. He will, in every human way, appeal to the best idea of society. But his profound comprehension and irresistible presence will be the result of an invisible network of thousands of years of collective knowledge. He will represent the embodiment of a very old and superintelligent spirit. As Jesus Christ was the "seed" of the woman, he will be the "seed" of the serpent" (Gen 3.15). Although his arrival in the form of a man was foretold by numerous scriptures, the broad masses of the world will not recognize him as the ultimate transgenic incarnation—the "beast" of Revelation 13.1.

It has been assumed for centuries that a prerequisite for the coming of the Antichrist would be the "revived" world order of Daniel's prophecy—an umbrella under which national boundaries dissolve, and ethnic groups, ideologies, religions, and economics from around the world, orchestrate a single and dominant sovereignty. Such a system will supposedly be free of religious and political extremes, and membership will tolerate the philosophical and cultural differences of its constituents. Except for minor nonconformity, war, intolerance, and hunger will be a thing of the past. At the head of the utopian administration, a single personality will surface. He will appear to be a man of distinguished character, but will ultimately become "a king of fierce countenance" (Dan. 8.23). With imperious decree he will facilitate a one-world government, a universal religion, and global socialism. Those who refuse his New World Order will inevitably be imprisoned or destroyed, until at last he exalts himself "above all that is called God, or that is worshiped, so that he, as God, sitteth in the temple of God, showing himself that he is God" (2 Thess. 2.4).

For many years the idea that such an "Orwellian" society would arise—where a one-world government oversees the smallest details of our lives and where human liberties are abandoned—was considered an anathema. The concept that rugged individualism could be sacrificed for an anesthetized universal harmony was repudiated by America's greatest minds. Then, in the 1970s, things began to change. Following a call by Nelson Rockefeller for the creation of a "new world order," presidential candidate Jimmy Carter campaigned, saying, "We must replace balance of power politics with world order politics." Evidently he struck a chord with world leaders. During the 1980s President George Bush, Sr. continued the one-world dirge by announcing over national television that "a new world order" had arrived. Following the initial broadcast, President Bush addressed the Congress and made the additional comment:

> What is at stake is more than one small country [Kuwait], it is a big idea—a new world order, where diverse nations are drawn together in common cause to achieve the universal aspirations of mankind: peace and security, freedom, and the rule of law. Such is a world worthy of our struggle, and worthy of our children's future! (Robertson 5)

Ever since the President's astonishing newscast, a parade of political and religious leaders have discharged a profusion of rhetoric aimed at implementing the goals of the New World Order. Concurrent with the political aspects of the NWO is the syncretistic and spiritual goals of New Agers and Dominionists. The blending of politics and spirituality, such as occurs in these movements, harmonizes perfectly with the ideas of an end-time marriage of government policy and religious creed as was prophesied in the Bible. To that end, the tools necessary for paganism's ultimate incarnation—the god-king of the Great Tribulation (Satan in flesh)—are in place. The "gods" have been revived through modern mysticism. The pagan agenda of governing by "divine representation" is being constructed. The governments of the world are uniting beneath a one-world banner, and the earth's masses stand at the brink of a decisive moment in time.

According to some Christians, this is the unfolding of an ancient scheme. At the core of the conspiracy, a leader of indescribable brutality is scheduled to appear. He will make the combined depravities of Antiochus Epiphanes, Hitler, Stalin, and Genghis Khan, all of whom were types of the Antichrist, look like Pee Wee Herman's Playhouse. He will raise his fist, "speaking great things…in blasphemy against God, to blaspheme his name, and his tabernacle, and them that dwell in heaven" (Rev. 13.5-6). As he champions worship of the gods who comes through portals, he will cause "that as many as would not worship the image of the beast should be killed" (Rev. 13.15). "The King of Babylon," as he is called in Isaiah 14, will revive the Babylonian mystery religion—"the habitation of devils, and the hold of every foul spirit, and a cage of every unclean and hateful bird" where merchants of the earth trade in "souls of men" and where "the blood of prophets, and of saints" is found (Rev. 18.2, 13, 24).

The book of Revelation details what follows the rise of Antichrist, culminating in cataclysmic war called Armageddon, a time during which God Almighty judges the "gods" who come through portals, including, we would assume, so-called Zeus, Apollo, Demeter, Isis, and others.

However futile, the gods will retaliate, and a war of indescribable intensity will occur. It will be fought on land and sea, in the heavens above, and in the earth below, in the physical and spiritual worlds. It will include "Michael and his angels [fighting] against the dragon; and the dragon [fighting] and his angels" (Rev. 12.7). Some humans will join the battle against God, calling on "idols of gold, and silver, and brass, and stone, and of wood" (Rev. 9.20) to convene their power against the Christian God, even uniting with "unclean spirits like frogs…the spirits of devils [the frog goddesses Heka?] working miracles, which go forth unto the kings of the earth…to gather them to the battle of that great day…[to] a place called in the Hebrew tongue Armageddon ["Mount Megiddo"]" (Rev. 16.13-14,16). There, in the valley of Megiddo, the omnipotent Christ will utterly repel the forces of darkness and destroy the New World army. Blood will flow like rivers, and the fowl of the air will "eat the flesh of the mighty, and drink the blood of the princes of the earth" (Ezek. 39.18). Besides Armageddon, battles will be fought in the Valley of Jehoshaphat and in the city of Jerusalem. Yet, the battle of Armageddon is the event that culminates the hostility between God Almighty and the lower gods that traverse portals.

Once before, Satan and his "god" spirits, challenged Yahweh at Megiddo. They lost. On Mount Carmel, overlooking the Valley of Armageddon, the prophets of Baal dared the Hebrew God to answer by fire. He did, and it looks like he will again. When he does, here is what the Bible says will happen:

> And I saw the beast, and the kings of the earth, and their armies, gathered together to make war against him that sat on the horse [Jesus], and against his army. And the beast was taken, and with him the false prophet that wrought miracles before him, with which he deceived them that had received the mark of the beast, and them that worshipped his image. These both were cast alive into a lake of fire burning with brimstone. And the remnant were slain with the sword of him that sat upon the horse, which sword proceeded out of his mouth: and all the fowls were filled with their flesh….And I saw a great white throne, and him that sat on it, from whose face the earth and the heaven fled away: and there was found no place [to hide]. And I saw the dead, small and great, stand before God; and the books were opened: and another book was opened, which is the book of life: and the dead were judged out of those things which were written in the books, according to their works…And

whosoever was not found written in the book of life was cast into the lake of fire." (Rev.19.19-21; 20.11-12,15)

A different destiny awaits the righteous following the battle of Armageddon:

And I saw heaven opened, and behold a white horse; and he that sat upon him was called Faithful and True [Jesus], and in righteousness he doth judge and make war. His eyes were as a flame of fire, and on his head were many crowns; and he had a name written, that no man knew, but he himself. And he was clothed with a vesture dipped in blood: and his name is called The Word of God. And the armies which were in heaven followed him upon white horses, clothed in fine linen, white and clean. And out of his mouth goeth a sharp sword, that with it he should smite the nations: and he shall rule them with a rod of iron: and he treadeth the winepress of the fierceness and wrath of Almighty God. And he hath on his thigh a name written, KING OF KINGS, AND LORD OF LORDS.... And I saw a new heaven and a new earth: for the first heaven and the first earth were passed away; and...I heard a great voice out of heaven saying, Behold, the tabernacle of God is with men....And God shall wipe away all tears from their eyes; and there shall be no more death, neither sorrow, nor crying, neither shall there be any more pain: for the former things are passed away. And he that sat upon the throne said...I will give unto him that is athirst of the fountain of the water of life freely. He that overcometh shall inherit all things; and I will be his God, and he shall be my son [or daughter]. (Rev. 19.11-16; 20.1-7)

Chapter 14

OTHER VIEWS
AND SUMMARY

The copy of the Genesis Apocryphon discovered at Qumran dates back to the second century B.C.... When discovered in 1947, it had been much mutilated from the ravages of time and humidity.... When scholars finally made public its content, the document confirmed that celestial beings from the skies had landed on planet Earth. More than that, it told how these beings had mated with Earth-women and had begat giants. (Thomas 84)

E ven a casual perusal of the information we have surveyed over the various parts of this book should be enough to convince most people that something credible and possibly of religious and historical value has occurred since the dawn of time. Many, including a number of secular researchers, believe this activity—often referred to in this book as UFO Phenomenon—is, in many cases, identical to biblical demonology. Millions of people also see the UFOs of modern times combined with alien abduction activity and emerging sciences such as cloning and transgenics as forecasting a coming hybrid (ET?) world leader, which some Christians fear could be the False Christ.

Others disagree with this assessment and believe the UFO manifestations are, by and large, equivalent to religious mythology that possibly point to a return of "creator beings" who visited earth in the remote past, improved hominid DNA, and accelerated human evolution.

George King says information was "telepathically relayed" to him from a superintelligence concerning a coming global leader (King 68). In his book *The Day the Gods Came*, he writes:

There will shortly come Another among you. He will stand tall among men with a shining countenance. This One will be attired in a single garment of the type now known to you....His magic will be greater than any upon Earth—greater than the combined materialistic might of all the armies. And they who heed not his words shall be removed from the Earth ...there will be no mystery about the birth of the next world Avatar as there was about the birth of Krishna, Buddha, Jesus and others. This majestic Being will come among men dressed in the one piece suit usually worn by the Intelligences from other Planets....He will have great powers which, by Karmic Law, He will be allowed to use in order to demonstrate to all men beyond all doubt, the Authority empowering Him to carry out His great Mission on Earth.... The power of this Being will be greater than mankind has ever seen before...as to be almost terrible, for..."They who heed not His words, shall be removed from the Earth." (King 68)

King's beliefs—that a coming world Avatar is scheduled to appear—is accepted by millions of people around the world who likewise look for an alien savior.

Whitley Strieber foresaw the credible appearance of ET as the dawn of a new religion:

It is a social issue of the utmost importance, because it has all the potential of a truly powerful idea to enter unconscious mythology and there to generate beliefs so broad in their scope and deep in their impact that they emerge with religious implications for the surrounding culture. The only thing now needed to make the UFO myth a new religion of remarkable scope and force is a single undeniable sighting. (Vallee)

Official Disclosure could pave the way for a new religion according to Jacques Vallée:

I think the stage is set for the appearance of new faiths, centered on the UFO belief. To a greater degree than all the phenomena modern science is confronting, the UFO can inspire awe, the sense of the smallness of man, and an idea of the possibility of contact with the cosmic. The religions we have briefly surveyed began with the miraculous experiences of one person, but today there are thousands for whom belief in other-worldly contact is based on intimate conviction, drawn from what they regard as personal contact with UFOs and their occupants. (Vallée 192)

Yet, Vallée senses malevolence in this "salvation from above." In his book *Messengers of Deception: Ufo Contacts and Cults*, he says:

I believe there is a machinery of mass manipulation behind the UFO phenomenon. It aims at social and political goals by diverting attention from some human problems and by providing a potential release for tensions caused by others. The contactees are a part of that machinery. They are helping to create a new form of belief: an expectation of actual contact among large parts of the public. In turn this expectation makes millions of people hope for the imminent realization of that age-old dream: salvation from above, surrender to the greater power of some wise navigators of the cosmos. (Vallée 20)

The effect of ET disclosure on Christians has been an issue for more than forty years among those in government with access to UFO information. The issue raised by the sudden appearance of unknown flying craft and occupants of unknown superior intellect could shake the foundations of religious paradigms and irreversibly alter the biblical worldview.

UFO researcher Richard Boylan says of this:

One of the predictions is that there will be a very large rift in human society as a result of ET contact becoming publicly known....The Aviary [a super-secret group of government and military officials according to Boylan] are quite concerned that fundamentalist Christians will experience spiritual, if not ontological, shock at the revelation of ET visitation...the theological and religious social implications may be the most serious ones resulting from open extraterrestrial contact..." (Missler and Eastman 298)

The Aviary were reportedly alarmed last year when stories appeared then quickly vanished about Vatican experts briefing government representatives from several countries on the Fatima Prophecies and what was alleged to be descriptions of ET visitations. According to Boylan, a spokesman for the Vatican verified that the briefing took place. Recent press from Vatican officials confirms the Catholic Church's interest in and concern for the effect upon the world's religions by Official ET Disclosure. Catholics are being reassured by church theologians including José Funes, Monsignor Corrado Balducci and astronomer Guy Consolmagno that ETs "… are God's creatures and no challenge to Rome's authority" (Mackay). In fact, Consolmagno says, "The discovery of extraterrestrial life…might…help us discard the bad ideas in religion—the narrow views, the hubris, the divisiveness" (Mackay).

Some of Consolmagno's views, especially where he interprets the first chapter of the book of John as meaning that "…the word of God—the spirit of the essence, the meaning of God—existed before anything else, and is part of everything in the natural universe: even a giant mindworm on a planet orbiting Alpha Centauri" (Mackay) are seen as variations on the Star Wars Jedi Ascended Masters Theology, animism, and pantheism.

Dr. Daniel Noel, professor of liberal studies in religion and culture at Norwich University in Montpelier, Vermont, wrote a thesis a few years ago about such theological migrations away from orthodoxy and toward a "God is all and all is God" worldview. In an article called, "Why the X-Files is Becoming Our New Religion," Christopher Guly points to Noel's research as proof that a growing number of the world's religions are warming up to an X-Files-UFO-Star-Wars Ascended Masters belief system, which, as he sees it, would eventually transplant traditional faith in the United States and warm people to accept the coming extraterrestrial religion. (Guly)

Those who worry about church authorities making

such dogmatic leaps believe this will play into the hands of what Vallée warns about in *Messengers of Deception* and ultimately towards a global leader who will lead the "final world government."

In *The Fellowship*, Brad Steiger puts his finger on this point:

> The Space Beings seem very concerned with the spreading of what has come to be known as New Age concepts....The Space Beings appear definitely concerned with seeing that all humankind is united as "one" on this planet....Contactees have been told that the Space Beings hope to guide Earth to a period of great unification, when all races will shun discriminatory separations and all of humankind will recognize its responsibility to every other life form existing on the planet. The Space Beings also seek to bring about a single, solidified government, which will conduct itself in spiritual principles and permit all of its citizens to grow constructively in love. (Steiger 51)

Lord Hill-Norton, who died last year at the age of eighty-nine, was an Admiral of the British Fleet and Chairman of the NATO Military Committee. In his later years he became transparent about what he knew and about what he suspected regarding UFOs. He felt the religion of ET was "definitely antithetical to orthodox Christian belief" and potentially a Satanic setup (Clarke). The February 28, 1997, edition of *The London Times* reports Gordon Creighton of *Flying Saucer Review* as agreeing with Lord Hill-Norton that, "...the great bulk of these phenomena are what is called Satanic" (Clarke).

THE "OTHER THEM"

Alien intelligence that appears to come through portals offer a disturbing challenge for people from different worldviews. The vast majority of true contactees and especially abductees find experience with the unknowns terrifying and ultimately undesirable. Like the Assyrians who built magic gateways to filter out evil supernaturalism, anything that might negate the infernal sense of coming face to face with *them* is ardently sought after. During the ascendancy of Nazi Germany, Rauschning, the Governor of Danzig related a strange episode in which Hitler had "a being" that came after him from the unknown. The incident was quite reminiscent of the paralysis and sense of foreboding acquainted with modern "alien" abduction reports:

> A person close to Hitler told me that he wakes up in the night screaming and in convulsions. He calls for help, and appears to be half paralyzed. He is seized with a panic that makes him tremble until the bed shakes. He utters confused and unintelligible sounds, gasping, as if on the point of suffocation. The same person described to me one of these fits, with details that I would refuse to believe had I not complete confidence in my informant.
>
> Hitler was standing up in his room, swaying and looking all round him as if he were lost. "It's he, it's he," he groaned, "he's come for me!" His lips were white; he was sweating profusely. Suddenly he uttered a string of meaningless figures, then words and scraps of sentences. It was terrifying. He used strange expressions strung together in bizarre disorder. Then he relapsed again

into silence, but his lips still continued to move. He was then given a friction and something to drink. Then suddenly he screamed: "There! there! Over in the comer! He is there!"—all the time stamping with his feet and shouting. To quieten him he was assured that nothing extraordinary had happened, and finally he gradually calmed down. After that he slept for a long time and became normal again... (Rausching).

The sheer terror felt when autonomy is so rudely interrupted by beings who manifest through slits in the fabric of space-time is not something non-experiencers (as they are known in Ufology) can or should pretend to understand. We weakly imagine the occurrences to be comparable to those who have been, in the course of supernatural warfare, met face to face with insidious forces so dark that they dare not think of them after the fact or recall vanquished details of their memories and presence. In all my life and during the few experiences I had with exorcism, unexplainable examples of superhuman strength yielded troubling phenomena, some of which were never fully explained to me; yet, the greatest encounter I had with Darkness by far and which I may document when the time is right, was a case study in the realm of demonic power so powerful as to be thought of as second only to Satan himself. In this instance, the spirit was confronted on more than one occasion by my staff, my family, and myself while we were in the employ of the largest evangelical organization in the world. Though the demon wielded significant influence among members of the organization and its leaders, it actually lived in the woods (also significant) and called itself a "spirit of religion." The supernatural hostility it possessed was incomprehensible. We were thankful to escape alive. This spirit and others like it compass the world to make one proselyte "then make it twofold more a child of hell" than they are themselves (Mt. 23.15). These incredibly smart hostiles nourish Christ-less attitudes among many church-goers and fill them with apathy toward the infirmed, so that those who need ministry the most are denied it. The loneliness thus felt by abduction experiencers, for instance, leaves them feeling hopeless, as if they are unfavored and unblessed. Yet, the life of Jesus reveals that God has devotion for those rejected by spirits and institution leaders. He has "other them," multi-dimensionals of equal and greater power we call angels. The writers of the early church, including Origen and Eusebius believed that every person is accompanied by a personal guardian angel. The followers of Christ evidently held such a view, for when Peter stood outside knocking on the door at Mary's house, they said, "It is his angel" (Acts 12.15). This is certainly true of children according to Matthew 18.10. And during 'abduction' situations, some have reported that praying to God for his angels to surround their homes and protect them has succeeded in halting the abduction phenomenon.

Due to the popularity of certain Ufology positions focusing on the contrast between Christian-Prophetic and Ancient Astronaut theories—we have not committed time to studying lesser known theorems in this book. In no particular order, a few of the examples we chose not to include are:

1. Superstitious Designations?

The proponents of this thought believe that UFO/aliens do not exist except in the imagination. They argue that man's early habit of blaming natural diseases, catastrophes, and seasons on the activity of "gods" illustrates a psychological fallacy. In some cases conditions such as sleep paralysis have also been shown to produce conditions similar to alien abduction reports.

This theory is not entirely without merit. The human imagination can be persuasive. Our minds convince us that natural wonders are the presence of ghostly or alien beings. Some people take medication to control such wandering thoughts, a remedy one would consider powerless if indeed all such ET phenomena were real.

Yet, since theories such as sleep paralysis do not explain the redundant manifestations reported by tens of thousands of unrelated witnesses, this theory is considered incomplete by most Ufologists.

2. Spirits of a Pre-Adamic Race?

Those holding this concept believe a pre-Adamic race existed on the original earth before it became "dark and void" (Gen. 1.2). These humanlike beings lived under the government of God, and were presided over by Lucifer, the "anointed cherub that covereth" (Ezek. 28.14). When these pre-Adamites joined Lucifer in a revolt against God, a cataclysm of darkness fell upon the earth, physically destroying its human-like inhabitants. Only the spirits of these creatures survived to roam the earth disembodied. This is supposed to explain the apparent desire of demons to possess human bodies and/or the need of aliens to harvest human DNA.

3. Spirits of Wicked People Deceased

This seems to be a perversion of Greek mythology. For instance, the Homeric Gods, who were but supernatural men, were both good and evil. The hypothesis here includes the idea that good and powerful spirits of good men rose up to assume places of deity after experiencing physical death, while the evil spirits of deceased evil men were gods who roamed the earth and its interior. At death, some of these spirits remained in an eternal limbo, unable to perish, yet incapable of attaining heaven or Olympus. Such is used to establish the idea that demons/ET are the spirits of wicked men deceased while "good" people become angels.

4. Heiser's Lion

The first person to have brought the following unusual archetype for UFO/ET interpretation to me, which suggests that ET may be an intelligent being similar to an unknown animal, was Dr. Michael Heiser. Therefore, I commonly refer to this theory as "Heiser's Lion."

When I asked Dr. Heiser to respond to the hypothetical question, "What if ET behaves in a fallen manner, wouldn't that indicate that he is demonic? Sinful?" Heiser responded to me via email this way:

Taking the latter first, we would only use words like "sin" if the one doing the action was morally culpable, which ET [may not be]. When a dog attacks a child, we don't say he sinned. We DO say, however (and this goes to the first part of the objection) the dog did what it did as a general (awful) byproduct of the Fall. Creatures are not morally guilty, but they do act violently because of the Fall. Therefore, if ET is not a demon but still does violent things, it is a result of the Fall—but it doesn't require a separate atonement for ET.

5. Classified Government Experiments

Not long ago Dr. Mike Heiser (Ph.D. in Biblical Hebrew and Ancient Semitic Languages) wrote a review forRaidersNews Network.com of Nick Redfern's book—*Body Snatchers in the Desert: The Horrible Truth at the Heart of the Roswell Story*, which offered a very human explanation for the Roswell event—essentially the same as Heiser had put forth in his book *The Facade* some years earlier—that the bodies connected with the Roswell event were human unfortunates used by "sanitized Nazis" crawling through the corridors of our nation's defense and aerospace industries. Some add to the "Operation Paperclip" screw up, Japan's Unit 731 atrocities, NEPA human test subjects, and other possibilities, the idea that, in some cases, "alien" abductions were the product of government mind control experiments or governments acting in league with extraterrestrials.

SUMMARY

We conclude in this book that:

- Redundant mythos have existed since the beginning of time consistent with modern UFO phenomena.
- Cargo cults and deity-myths around the world repeat the story of earth visitation by superintelligent beings who involved themselves with manipulating human DNA.
- Beings of myth were at least at times based on authentic interaction with superintelligences of unknown origin.
- Certain mythology as well as anomalous "historical records" were the efforts of men to interpret these eyewitness accounts and visitations.
- These beings were/are seen as traversing gateways, portals, dimensional openings, and ladders from air, sea, and earth.
- Bible scholars agree that sky, sea, and physical earth contain forces behind barriers or "gates."
- In Genesis 6 the "sons of God" produced a race of offspring called *Nephilim*. In the New Testament, Jesus

spoke of these days (of Noah) as being comparable to the time leading up to his return and of the end of the age. (Luke 17.26-27)

- The Egyptians originally migrated from the biblical land of *Shin'ar*, which means the *Land of the Watchers*. The Egyptians called it *Ta Neter*—"The Land of the Watchers"—"from which the gods came into Egypt." These Watchers are identified as powerful angels which descended from Heaven to earth and produced the giant nephilim.

- In the *Book of the Dead* there are prayers for deliverance from the Watchers (*Tchatcha*, the princes of Osiris), who came from *Ta-Ur*, the "Far Away Land."

- The Sumerian scribes referred to the Watchers as *Anunnaki*, which, they said, "came from *Nibiru*" to judge/rule the inhabitants of the earth. Some interpret this Nibiru as "a distant planet," while others say it should be translated, "Those Who from Heaven to Earth Came."

- In the *Book of Jubilees*—a.k.a. the *Apocalypse of Moses*—the Watchers are compared to supernatural beings mentioned in the sixth chapter of Genesis.

- An intelligent, functioning dynamic exists beyond or behind other mythology, which according to Christian doctrine is identical with legions of fallen spiritual forces held within spiritual boundaries.

- When contact with these forces have been desired, beings of startling similarity have materialized from sky, sea, or beneath the earth's surface.

- One of the more disturbing aspects of the "beings who breach the gate," is "abduction," which continues to be reported around the world.

- Occultists who have sought to bridge the dimensional vortex between the world of seen and unseen have sometimes experienced beings strikingly similar to alien "Greys," "reptilians," etc.
- Occultists as well as scholars find repetition with regard to these beings and Babylon.
- "The Ancient Astronaut" theory claims that super-intelligent beings have been visiting the earth through dimensional gates for eons. These are "the gods of mythology" and responsible for creating the human species.
- Gateways (stargates) were represented on earth in Assyrian and other archways built through elaborate construction ceremonies and blessed by names of good omens.
- Colossal transgenic creatures stood guard at the gates and palace entries to keep undesirable forces from coming through the portals—important imitative magic thought to represent heavenly ideas—guardians that were often accompanied by winged spirits holding magic devices and magic statuettes concealed beneath floors.
- Winged-discs are universally associated with the flying gods mythos.
- Pyramidal shapes around the world are connected to the myth of flying serpent gods and the portals or openings they come through.
- Some of the myths involving flying serpent gods include prophecy of their return through heaven's gates at the end of time.
- Other deities—such as Zeus—were associated with the sky, the prince of the air, and the biblical fall of Lucifer.

- Hesiod's *Theogony*, Homer's *Iliad*, and the Bible characterize the place of imprisoned rebel angels using the same words—Tartarus and the Bottomless Pit.
- Imitative magic—based on deeply held ancient beliefs about orcas, pits, and containers—sought through mystery rituals to incarnate these "gods" through dimensional openings.
- The earth as well as moons of "outer darkness" were perceived as prisons containing rebel spirits.
- Two wormhole-stargates were envisioned as positioned at the beginning and ending points of the sky where the ecliptic, the pathway of the sun, crosses the Milky Way.
- Universal descriptions depict the distance between these points as a snake encompassing the heavens.
- Often, beings are depicted entering the mouth of the snake—iconography some view as a record of arrival and departure of superintelligent beings using wormholes (stargates) to navigate the heavens.
- In other renderings a ladder is seen descending from the ecliptic providing a connecting point between earth and heaven, such as in Jacob's ladder and similar extra-biblical accounts.
- Teachings about traversable "Gates of Heaven" were understood by early Christians, and some believe St. Peter's appointment as "gate-keeper" is a reference to the belief.
- Evidence that Jesus himself referred to these gates is viewed by some in places such as Matt. 7.14 and 16.18.
- One of the most important aspects of the universal serpent-Stargate imagery connecting both ends of the

Milky Way has to do with the year 2012, and the prophesied "end of times" reopening of the serpent portal.

- The end of the great cycle of the Maya calendar and the 26,000 year planetary cycle of the Aztec calendar is December 21, 2012.

- According to *The Bible Code* by Michael Drosnin, the world will end on this date due to a collision with a meteor, asteroid or comet. Another theory—the "Novelty Theory"—claims time itself is a "fractal wave," which will end abruptly in 2012. Even the popular television program—*X-Files*—speculated that colonization of the earth by "aliens" would occur in December 2012.

- The Maya tell of Quetzalcoatl, the Feathered Serpent (according to some, "feathered" equates to flying technology while "serpent" refers to the heavenly wormhole-Stargate) descending through a "hole in the sky" on a rope ladder (another version of the descending-Quetzalcoatl myth describes him sailing down on a winged ship). They prophecy in 2012 this "serpent rope" will emerge again from the center of the Milky Way and Quetzalcoatl will return at this end of time.

- Some wonder, if Quetzalcoatl returns December 21, 2012, does this imply anything for those who believe in a seven-year period of Great Tribulation? Or those who believe in a mid-tribulation 'rapture' of the church?

- Students of comparative religions find corresponding legends from around the world combining imagery of heavenly (or elevated) serpents, bearded saviors, and the beginning of creation and ending of time based on the return of the "one."

- The Bible makes the case that gateways can be opened over cities and/or countries that allow good and/or evil influences to dominate those geographies.
- Others interpret these historical depictions, records, and myths differently than do Hebrew scriptures.
- Both secular and religious Ufologists interpret the beings who come through dimensional gateways as associated with UFO phenomenon and as equal in many cases to biblical demonology.
- Dimensional gateways might actually be an unknown form of Holography.
- Dimensional gateways could also point to traversable wormholes.
- In order to materialize and take definite form, these entities seem to require a source of energy; a fire or a living thing—plant, a tree, a human medium (or contactee).
- Perhaps that is why dogs and animals tend to vanish in UFO flap areas. Perhaps the living cells of those animals are somehow used by the ultraterrestrials to create forms, which we can see and sense with our limited three-dimensional perceptions.
- Some interpret this activity as the morphogenesis of demons.
- Although the Bible warns of communicating with familiar spirits, consulting mediums, or otherwise offering invitations to other-dimensional entities, the revival of ancient oracles and the experiences drawn from them are especially seductive curiosities to followers of modern Ufology and spiritualism.

- Contemporary reports lead researchers to believe the ancient myths and prophecies may have described current unfolding events as portending a last days opening of the gates and the return of the "creator."
- Some Christians believe this is aimed at preparing the earth for an extraterrestrial "visitation of the gods," and, more importantly, at changing the world's religious beliefs.
- Around the world an interesting story is repeated about "the god" of heaven warring with "the dragon" of the sea during both the beginning and ending of time.
- Parallels between "angels," "demons," and ET phenomena are increasingly recognized by experts of different fields of Ufology.
- More and more question the *mechanized* "nuts-and-bolts" approach to defining UFO phenomena in favor of "spiritual conceptualization" of ET.
- This aspect of UFO phenomena is almost inevitably tied to generational "abduction" scenarios and often includes occult practices and belief.
- Given that most experts—religious and secular—agree on this important point: that often the beings who come through portals (demons or ET) are one and the same—the question is begged, "What are these creatures up to?"
- The answer seems to revolve around alleged abduction and hybrid-breeding.
- The familiar Genesis story of Watchers cohabiting with women parallels the modern "abduction" reports in that the "...sons of God...took them wives of all which they chose" (Gen. 6.2).

- The implication here is that, as in alien abduction, this was not by mutual agreement or harmony of wills, but that these women were taken ("took") forcibly at the sole discretion of the powerful beings. As a result of the abduction-marriages, hybrids were born of the genetic interruption called "Nephilim."

- From the Middle Ages forward, many church leaders have believed that the Antichrist would ultimately be conceived through demoniality—the union of a demon and a human.

- If the Antichrist is in fact at length the physical offspring of a demon, not only will he be the exact opposite of Jesus (son of God), but the forerunner of the return of the Nephilim.

- Isaiah (chapters 13 and 14) tied the return of the Nephilim to the destruction of Babylon (Iraq) in the end of days.

- One also notes with regard to the "mighty ones" and their connection with Babylon, that when "... Cush begat Nimrod: he began to be a *mighty one* in the earth... . And the beginning of his kingdom was *Babel...*" [emphasis added] (Gen 10.8-10). Thus, Babylon began with the Nephilim and/or Gibborim.

- The Tower of Babel may have had a Stargate opening above it, allowing for higher dimensional beings to descend slowly while dissipating energy.

- The relationship between Babylon (the gate god) and the first giants, as well as Babylon and these returning giants, is stunning in light of recent global activity, biotechnology, and the US invasion of Babylon (Iraq).

- In the tenth chapter of Daniel, the prophet struggles in prayer against Ahriman, the "prince of Persia" or gatekeeper of Babylon.
- Throughout the Bible, spiritual Babylon is equivalent to the world system that is at enmity with God. Babylon began at the Tower of Babel, where at the macro level Satan first attempted his strategy to incarnate a one-world system.
- Daniel's divine prediction about the last world empire is amazing in light of the extraordinary references made in Chapter 2: "And whereas thou sawest iron mixed with miry clay, they shall mingle themselves with the seed of men: but they shall not cleave one to another, even as iron is not mixed with clay" (Dan. 2.43).
- The personal pronoun, "*they* shall mingle themselves with the seed of men…" (Dan 2.43) forces the question, "Who are the 'non-seed' that are 'mingling with the seed of men?"
- The mingling of seed is related to "vital energy" or created matter used by ultradimensionals to format a body that they may use to enter the third dimension.
- Daniel's prophecy, coupled with Genesis Chapter 3, provides an incredible tenet—that Satan has <u>seed</u>, and <u>it</u> is at enmity with Christ (Gen 3.15).
- The word translated here as "seed" is the Hebrew word *zera,* which means "offspring, descendants, children."
- According to the Bible, the Antichrist will be "the son of perdition," the male progeny of the Greek *apoleia,* or Apollyon. The implication is that the Man of Sin will be the physical offspring of the destroyer demon, a transgenic of the highest order.

- Some disagree with the inferences and conclusions of *Nephilim Stargates: The Year 2012 and the Return of the Watchers* interpreting the phenomena studied in this book as possibly: 1) Advanced extraterrestrial or multidimensional intelligence; 2) Superstitious Designations; 3) Spirits of a Pre-Adamic Race; 4) Spirits of Wicked People Deceased; 5) Heiser's Lion; and/or 6) Classified Government Experiments.

To contact Tom Horn please visit *RaidersNewsNetwork.com*

Works Cited

"Amalantrah Working," The [Liber XCVII], Original key entry by Fr. H. B. in New York 4/12/90 e.v. ASCII conversion by Bill Heidrick, T.G. of O.T.O., Copyright (c) Ordo Templi Orientis. <http://www. luckymojo.com/esoteric/occultism/magic/ceremonial/crowley/ 097amalantrah.txt>.

Apuleius, Lucius. *The Golden Asse.* Trans. Adlington, 1566.

Augustine, St. *City of God.*

Bartholomew, Courtenay, M.D. *Fatima's Solar Miracle: A Nuclear Prophecy?*: Mother of All Peoples, 2006.

Booth, Billy. "UFOs on the Moon 3," About.com <http://ufos.about. com/od/nasaufos/p/ufosmoon3.htm>.

Budge, Wallis E. A. *Legends of the Gods: The Egyptian Texts.*

Capelotti, P .J. "Space: The Final [Archaeological] Frontier." *Archaeology Magazine* 57. 6 (2004) <http://www.archaeology. org/0411/etc/space.html>.

Case Western Reserve University <http://www.medicalnewstoday.com/ medicalnews.php?newsid=42331>. Note: Case Law School receives $773,000 NIH grant to develop guidelines for genetic enhancement research: Professor Max Mehlman to lead team of law professors, physicians, and bioethicists in two-year project, April 28, 2006.

Cavendish, Richard. *Man, Myth and Magic: The Illustrated Encyclopedia of Mythology, Religion and the Unknown*: Marshall Cavendish Corp, 1983.

Charles, Jonathan. "US Marines Offer Babylon Apology." BBC News, 14 Apr. 2006.

Cid, Ana Luisa. *Mexico Security Camera UFO dubbed "UFO from Dimensional Doorway,"* Investigación del Lic. Jaime Maussan (www. jaimemaussan.tv) Translation (c) 2005.

Scott Corrales, Institute of Hispanic Ufology (IHU) <www.
ufocasebook.com/mexicosecurity.html+Mexico+Security+Camera+
UFO+dubbed+%22UFO+from+Dimensional+Doorway&hl=en&c
t=clnk&cd=1&gl=u>.

Clarke, David. "A Space-Age Demonology." *Fortean Times,* June 2006
<http://www.forteantimes.com/articles/211_ufosfromhell2.shtml>.

Consolmagno, Guy. *Intelligent Life in the Universe? Catholic Belief and
the Search for Extraterrestrial Intelligent Life.* Catholic Truth Society.

Crème, Benjamin. The Reappearance of the Christ and the Masters of
Wisdom.

Daniel, Alma, Timothy Wyllie, and Andrew Ramer. *Ask Your Angels:
A Practical Guide to Working with the Messengers of Heaven to
Empower and Enrich Your Life.* New York: Ballantine Books, 1992.

Davies, Eric W., Ph.D. Presentation. "Wormhole-Stargates:
Tunneling Through the Cosmic Neighborhood." MUFON 2001
International UFO Symposium, July 2001.

Delmas, Dr. Achille. *Hitler, essai de biographie psycho- pathologique.*
Paris: Lib. Marcel, [Hermann Rauschning: Hitler m'a dit. Ed.
Co-operation, Paris, 1939. Dr. Achille Delmas: Hitler, essai de
biographie psycho- pathologique. Lib. Marcel Rivimere, Paris,
1946.].

Drosnin, Micahel. The Bible Code. New York: Touchstone Press,
1997.

Euripides. *The Bacchantes, Dramatis Personare [Messenger to Pentheus
concerning the Bacchantes].* Trans. Edward Philip Coleridge, 410
BC.

Floyd, Chris. "Monsters, Inc.: The Pentagon Plan to Create Mutant
'Super-Soldiers.'" CounterPunch <http://www.counterpunch.org/
floyd01132003.html>.

Flynn, David. *Cydonia: The Secret Chronicles of Mars.* Bozeman, MT:
End Time Thunder Publishers, 2002. --. E-mail to Tom Horn,
2005.

Forty. *Mythology: A Visual Encyclopedia.* London: PRC Publishing,
1999.

Fr. Ludovicus Maria Sinistrari de Ameno. *De Daemonialitate, et
Incubis, et Succubi.* Trans. Jacques Vallee in *Passport to Magonia.*
[New York]: Contemporary Books, 1993.

Glatz, Carol. "Do Space Aliens Have Souls? Inquiring Minds Can Check Jesuit's Book." *Catholic News Service*, VATICAN LETTER. Nov-4-2005 <http://www.catholicnews.com/data/stories/cns/0506301.htm>.

Gledhill, Ruth. "ET lives . . . and He's Christian." *The Times Online*, October 18, 2005 <http://www.watchermagazine.com/?p=1969>.

Greer, Steven M., MD. *Exopolitics or Xenopolitics?*. The Disclosure Project, 2 May 2006

Guly, Christopher. "Why the X-Files is Becoming Our New Religion." *The Ottawa Citizen*, March 5, 2000

Goldman, Stuart. *"They're Here!"* Letter sent to John Weldon, 29 Nov. 1989, and quoted in *The Facts on UFOs and Other Supernatural Phenomena* by Ankerberg and Weldon: Harvest Houst Publishers, 1992.

Goldsmith, Donald, and Tobias Owen. *The Search for Life in the Universe*. Menlo Park, CA: Benjamin/Cummings, 1980.

Good, Timothy. *Above Top Secret*. New York: William Morrow Co., 1988.

Grassie, William. *What Does It Mean to be Human?* A John Templeton Foundation Research Lecture Query, 2006 <http://www.templeton.org/milestones/milestones_2006-11.asp>.

Hall, Manly P. *The Secret Destiny of America.--. The Secret Teachings of All Ages*.

Heiser, Michael S., PhD. *Introduction to the Divine Council*. <http://www.thedivinecouncil.com/>.

Hesiod. *Theogony*. Trans. Evelyn-White.

Hillstrom, Elizabeth. *Testing the Spirits*. Downers Grove, IL: InterVarsity Press, 1995.

Hoagland, Richard. "Moon With a View: or, What Did Arthur Know . . . and When Did He "Know It?" *Enterprise Mission*. 2005. The Enterprise Mission, 23 July 2006 <http://www.enterprisemission.com/moon1.htm>.

Horn, Thomas and Nita Horn. *The Ahriman Gate*. Sisters, OR: Musterion Press, 2005.

Horn, Thomas R. and Donald C. Jones, PhD. *The Gods Who Walk Among Us*. Lafayette: Huntington House Publishers, 1999.

Horn, Thomas R. *Spiritual Warfare--The Invisible Invasion*. Lafayette: Huntington House Publishers, 1998.

Homer. *Hymns of Homer, The.* Trans. George Chapman, 1960. *Ice Giant Found In Siberia,* <http://www.museumofhoaxes.com/hoax/weblog/comments/ice_giant_found_in_siberia/>.

Kang, C.H., and Ethel R. Nelson. *The Discovery of Genesis.* St. Louis: Concordia Publishing House, 1979.

Kass, Leon R. *Life, Liberty and the Defense of Dignity: The Challenge for Bioethics.* Encounter Books, 2002.

Keel. *Operation Trojan Horse.* Illuminet Press, 1996.

Kennedy, James, PhD. *The Real Meaning of the Zodiac.* Ft. Lauderdale, FL: TCRM Publishing, 1993.

King, D.D. *The Day the Gods Came.* The Aetherius Society, 1965.

King, Francis. *Ritual Magic in England.* London: Neville Spearman, 1977.

Kinnaman, Gary. *Angels Dark and Light.* Ann Arbor, MI: Servant Publications, 1994.

Koch. *Christian Counseling and Occultism.* Grand Rapids: Kregel Publications, 1973.

Landsburg. *In Search of Ancient Mysteries.* New York: Bantam Books, 1974.

Lindsey, Hal. *Planet Earth: 2000 A.D. Will Mankind survive?.* Western Front Ltd, 1994.

Pauwells, Louis & Jacques Bergier. *The Dawn of Magic,* 1st published in France under the title *Le Matin des Magiciens.* Paris: Editions Gallimard, 1960.

Mack, John. *Abduction: Human Encounters with Aliens:* Ballantine Books, 1994.

Mackay, Neil. "And on the eighth day . . . Did God Create Aliens?" *The Sunday Herald.* 27 Nov. 2005 <http://findarticles.com/p/articles/mi_qn4156/is_20051127/ai_n15871821>.

Martin, Malachi. Interview with Art Bell. *Coast to Coast,* 05 Apr. 1997.

Missler, John and Mark Eastman. *Alien Encounters.* Coeur d'Alene, ID: Koinonia House, 1997.

Moody, Raymond and Paul Perry. *Reunions.* New York, NY: Villard Books, 1993.

Ohler, Shawn. "Hardly Alien Territory." *The Edmonton Journal.* (8 August 2006): 1 <http://www.canada.com/edmontonjournal/news/story.html?id=fb9f9103-05cf-47b5-a0c1-911f247c3060>.

Otto, Walter F. *Dionysus: Myth and Cult.* Indianapolis: Indiana University Press, 1965.

"Paranormal and occult hypotheses about UFOs." *Wikipedia, The Free Enclyclopedia.* 16 April. 2007.

Picken, Jane. "Medical Marvels." *The Evening Chronicle* 13 Apr. 2007.

Price. *The Angels Within Us: A Spiritual Guide to the Twenty-Two Angels that Govern Our Lives.* New York, NY: Fawcett/Columbine/ Ballantine, 1993.

Quayle, Steve. *Genesis 6 Giants.* Bozeman, MT: End Time Thunder Publishers, 2002.

Rauschning, Hermann. *Hitler m'a dit. Ed. Co-operation.* Paris, 1939.

Jamieson, Robert, A.R. Fausset, and David Brown. *Specific commentary by Jamieson on Isaiah 45 1-7,* Commentary Critical and Explanatory on the Whole Bible, 1871.

Robertson, Pat. *The New World Order.* Dallas, TX: Word Publishing, 1991.

Septuagint English Translation. Sir Lancelot Charles Lee Brenton. London: Samuel Bagster & Sons, Ltd., 1851.

Sitchin, Zecharia. "Sitchen and Vatican Theologian Discuss UFOs, Extraterrestrials, Angels, and Creation of Man." Dialogue in Bellaria <http://www.sitchin.com/vatican.htm>.

Steiger. *The Fellowship*: Doubleday, 1988.

Stokes, John. "Scientists Find Extraterrestrial Genes in Human DNA." *The Canadian.*

Strieber, Whitley. *Communion*: Beech Tree Books, 1987.--. Forward. *Dimensions:*
A Casebook of Alien Contact: Ballantine Books, 1989.

--. *Transformation*: Avon Books, 1988.

Suddock, Sally. "Priest says ETs are brethren." *Cosmiverse*, June 19, 2000.

Tanner, Adam SJ. *Tractatus Theologicus de Processu Adversus Crimina Excepta AC Speciatim Adversus Crimen Veenficii*: Cologne, 1629.

Tasker, R.V.G. "Our Lord's Use of the Old Testament." The Campbell Morgan Memorial Bible Lectureship, No. 5. Westminster Chapel, Buckingham Gate, London. 10 June 1953. 13. Biblical Studies.org. uk. <http://www.biblicalstudies.org.uk/article_ot_tasker.html>.

"Theurgy." *Wikipedia, The Free Enclyclopedia.* 17 July. 2006. Aug. 2006 <http://en.wikipedia.org/wiki/Theurgy>.

Thomas, I.D.E Dr. *The Omega Conspiracy.* Oklahoma City, OK: Hearthstone Publishing, 1986.

Thompson, Richard L. *Alien Identities: Ancient Insights into Modern UFO Phenomena.* Alachua, FL: Govardhan Hill Pub., 1993.

"Transhumanism." *Wikipedia: The Free Encyclopedia.* 2 May. 2007 <http://en.wikipedia.org/wiki/Transhumanism>.

Vallée, Jacques. *Confrontations.* Ballantine Books, 1990.

------. *Dimensions: A Casebook of Alien Contact.* Ballantine Books, 1989.

------. *The Invisible College.* New York: E.P.Dutton, 1975.

------. *Messengers of Deception.* And/Or Press, 1979.

------. *Passport to Magonia.* Chicago, IL: Contemporary Books Publishing, 1993.

------. *UFO's in Space: Anatomy of a Phenomenon.* New York: Ballantine Books, 1987.

van Buren, Elizabeth. *The Secret of the Illuminati.*

von Daniken, Erich. *Chariots of the Gods.* New York: G.P. Putnam's Sons, 1970.

Westcott, W. Wynn. *The Occult Power of Numbers.*